921

IGN

AUTHOR LIVERSEDGE, Douglas

TITLE IGNATIUS OF LOYOLA

DATE DUE	BORROWER'S NAME	ROOM NO.

921

ING

LIVERSEDGE, Douglas

IGNATIUS OF LOYOLA

IGNATIUS OF LOYOLA

IGNATIUS
OF LOYOLA

The Soldier-Saint

by DOUGLAS LIVERSIDGE

FRANKLIN WATTS, INC.
575 Lexington Avenue
New York, N.Y. 10022

3523

Other Immortals by the author
Lenin
Peter the Great
Saint Francis of Assisi
Joseph Stalin

Cover photograph courtesy
The New York Public Library

SBN 531 00939–4

Copyright © 1970 by Franklin Watts, Inc.
Library of Congress Catalog Card Number: 70-103098
Printed in the United States of America

CONTENTS

IGNATIUS OF LOYOLA

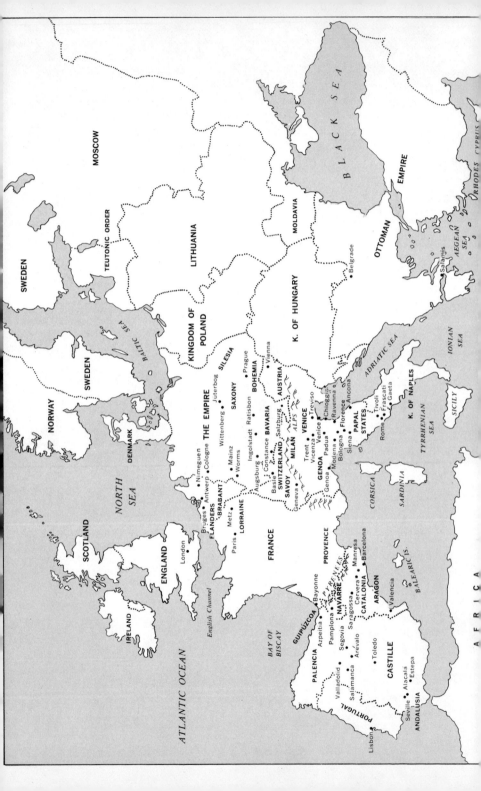

CHAPTER 1

THE EARLY YEARS

In the year 1522, on the eve of the Feast of the Annunciation, a soldier of fortune hung up his sword in the Church of Our Lady of Montserrat. He had resolved to serve God. Although he was unaware of it then, Ignatius de Loyola's simple act in that Spanish Pyrenean shrine was the first step toward founding a great religious movement—the Society of Jesus. One day Ignatius would lead a disciplined army for his captain, who was Christ. Sworn to poverty, and armed solely with the spirit of the Lord, his conquests would be many. Not the least would be those which would rid the Church of moral decay and stem the onrush of the Reformation.

On that historic night, just before commemorating the announcement to the Virgin Mary that she was to become the mother of Christ, Ignatius clad himself in the livery of his new calling. He knelt in prayer, wearing a gown of sackcloth. He had given his cavalier's clothes to a beggar, a gesture that symbolized the inflexible acceptance of poverty and a total break with worldliness. From now on, he would beg for his food in all humility, an experience that was alien to him, for he had been born into a noted family of great wealth.

Ignatius' father was Don Beltrán Jáñez de Oñaz y Loyola; his mother was Doña María Sáenz de Licona y Balda. Both parents were of high birth. Indeed, Don Beltrán, whose wealth was derived from estates and ironworks, belonged to that social elite which the monarch personally invited when the nobility rendered homage.

Little is known of Ignatius' boyhood and youth. In manhood he humbly confessed to having plundered an orchard, and there was also an incident involving himself and a brother in a tavern brawl. On his own admission, there were moments of imprudent wildness, for like many young men of his time, his morals were sometimes reprehensible and loose. He also had a fondness for sports and contests. In those carefree days, there was very little to suggest a future saint.

The birth year of Ignatius is uncertain. It is generally accepted as 1491, but some contend that it was four years later. In any event, he was born at the ancestral castle, which still exists about a mile from the little town of Azpeitia, in the Basque country of Spain. There, in the province of Guipúzcoa, the castle stands in its lonely valley, where the lower heights of the neighboring hills are decked with trees and bear traces of agriculture.

Ignatius was possibly the youngest of thirteen children: eight sons and five daughters. Whether or not those figures are correct, it is certain that he was the youngest son. Christened Iñigo after the canonized Abbot of Ona, years later he assumed the name Ignatius in tribute to the martyred bishop of Antioch. It seems likely that his mother, a pious woman, died during his childhood, for Don Beltrán sent him to Arévalo in old Castile, not far from Salamanca, to the home of Doña María de Guevara, an equally devout aunt. But it is doubtful that Doña María's piety influenced her charge, for Ignatius was soon removed to another household.

Although the reason for the move has never been made clear, Don Beltrán—apparently a man of worldly ambitions —sent Ignatius to live with an influential friend. Thus, the boy entered the home of Don Juan Velásquez de Cuéllar, the governor of Arévalo and an official of the royal treasury. Don Juan promised that Ignatius would eventually be placed in the king's household, thereby adding more distinction to the name of Loyola.

There was nothing unusual in this arrangement. Indeed, it was the practice of many well-to-do people to allow their young sons to work in the homes of powerful nobles. They served at table, lit the fires, made the beds, and fulfilled other menial tasks. So, Ignatius' social upbringing was essentially that of a self-indulgent courtier. He was taught to read and write, but beyond that he was unlettered. Later he revealed that he had sought pleasure—not a college, with its sobering environment. In fact, he was entirely given to the vanities of the world. Living in the manner of a gentleman, he especially "delighted in martial exercises, being led thereto by an ardent and innate desire of military glory."

As a young man, the sword and soldiery figured very strongly in Ignatius' life. And, apparently, so did poetry, for he wrote sonnets and canzones (lyric poems). Sometimes his verses had a religious flavor, but others were romantic. Ignatius never revealed the lady who was the object of his verses, other than that she was "not a countess nor a duchess but of a rank more exalted than either." If this were true, she could have been nothing less than a royal princess. It is speculated that she was Joanna, daughter of the queen-dowager of Naples and the niece of King Ferdinand.

During those youthful days, Ignatius, on his own admission, was guilty of sins, but he never said precisely what they were. No doubt the atmosphere of the Court at that period—with its rivalries, bickering, and braggarts—fostered incidents and escapades. And Ignatius, typical of many people of small stature—he was a little under five feet two —was ever ready to assert himself if provoked. An insult quickly roused him to anger, but his large features could just as swiftly be lit by good humor. His head was impressive, with its aquiline nose, forceful, arresting eyes, and thick, dark hair accentuating an unusually high forehead. Generosity and chivalry, as well as an insatiable desire for earthly glory, were his other traits.

Spaniards at that time were also generally captivated by weapons. As one observer recorded: ". . . the blast of trumpets in battle stirs them to the quick. It is my opinion, and that of many others, that they surpass all the nations in the art of war, notoriously by reason of bodily strength and agility, and heroism, and endurance of work, hunger and other necessary toils, but also because . . . they have great good sense." And through the years the family of Loyola had vigorously adhered to this military tradition. Ignatius' own brothers were courageous knights, and three would fall in battle.

Now, certain circumstances, as well as disenchantment with the ways of the Court, would change the young man's life. During 1516, the huge bell of Villila tolled for the death of King Ferdinand. It also announced the end of a chapter in Ignatius' career, for when his patron, Velásquez, died the following year, Ignatius decided to end what had become a pointless existence.

If Ignatius was born in 1491, he was twenty-six years old when he set out in search of military distinction. With him went 500 scudi (money of the time) and two horses that he had received from his patron's family.

The events that succeeded Ferdinand's death offered abundant scope to anyone who was inclined toward a military life. For years, battles had been fought bitterly over dynastic rights to Navarre, a northern independent province on the French border. Spain and France were mainly concerned with control of the strategic passes of the rugged Pyrenees.

After Ferdinand's death, the ousted king of Navarre, anxious to retrieve his throne, marched into his former kingdom with French forces. But the troops of the regent, the elderly Cardinal Ximénes, aided by the Duke of Nájera, viceroy of Navarre, drove them out. Castles were destroyed, and the fortification of the key city of Pamplona was begun. The French bided their time, and then struck fiercely when certain Spanish towns, fearing the loss of ancient liberties, rose against their young king, Charles V. Ignatius distinguished himself during these troubled times by capturing the Biscayan town of Nájera.

In the spring of 1521, the French, aware that Spanish troops had been withdrawn for their own civil war, once again invaded Navarre. First attacking St. Jean Pied de Port, a strong force then marched on Pamplona. The Duke of

7

Nájera hurried southward to try to raise reinforcements, leaving the small, inefficient garrison under the command of Francisco Herrera.

From the outset, there was little hope of defending the town. Cardinal Ximénes' plan for fortifying it had never been completed. There was also the attitude of the people to be reckoned with. Traditionally, the citizens tended to be biased toward whichever rival nation was not in control. Therefore, since Pamplona was garrisoned by Spaniards, the people rather cantankerously now favored the French. Herrera knew that his meager force would confront not only a mighty foe, but also hostile citizens.

Faced with overwhelming odds, Herrera thought it futile to fight. He told his brother officers that rather than a foolish waste of life, surrender was the sanest thing to do. But his words incensed the proud Ignatius. It would be cowardly, he argued, to submit. "I do not think even Aeneas worthy of admiration," he cried, "when I see him escaping from the flames that consumed his city; for to shun the common peril is the nature of cowards; to perish in the universal ruin is the mischance of brave men. I should hold him to deserve immortal glory if he had died a holocaust of his fidelity."

Finally, it was agreed to withdraw to the greater security of the citadel. As the French approached through the mountain passes, the Spanish realized how wise they had been to withdraw; the enemy was twelve thousand strong with thirty pieces of artillery.

A sketch of the critical situation is conveyed in a letter dated May 17, 1521, which relates: "The French are coming down the Roncal Valley in such numbers that they can't be counted. The towns round about rose yesterday for King Don Enrique [the claimant who was backed by France]; Pedro of Navarre, with the marshal's son, is at their head. The Duke of Nájera has hurried from Pamplona. The city is left to itself. The French army will be there tomorrow, and it is said that they need not unbuckle their spurs before taking the capital. . . . The whole kingdom is up for King Don Enrique, and the Duke of Nájera may thank God if he gets safe into Castile."

When Herrera failed to deal with the French, because the terms were unacceptable, the enemy quickly made their tactics known. They would breach the castle walls with intensive cannon fire to allow the infantry to rush in.

It was afternoon when the assault began. The guns roared from the neighboring streets, flinging their cannonballs at the barbican of the citadel. In comparison, the Spaniards' fire was feeble, and after a furious siege of some six or eight hours no one could have doubted the outcome.

During the battle, Ignatius was wounded. A heavy stone or a cannonball fractured his right leg and damaged the other. After he collapsed during those frantic moments on May 20, 1521, he would never again take up sword in battle.

Very soon the citadel fell to the French, but the enemy was not unchivalrous. Learning that the Spanish surgeon was dead, the French commander ordered his own doctors to tend Ignatius' wounds. For two weeks he lay in a house in the town before he was judged fit enough to leave Pamplona. No ransom was demanded, and so, leaving behind his helmet, sword, and shield, he was borne on a litter to his ancestral home.

9

Ignatius' father was dead, and had been succeeded by Don Martin Garcia, the eldest son, who was now fighting in Castile. The wounded Ignatius was greeted by his sister-in-law Magdalena, at one time a maid of honor to Queen Isabella.

As the days went by, it was obvious that Ignatius was making a poor recovery. The bones of his right leg were not well joined, and the wound was not healing quickly. When Don Martin came back to the castle, he sent for surgeons to examine his brother's leg. Their diagnosis was not encouraging. The only remedy was to break the leg once again and reset it. Unless this was done, Ignatius would be crippled.

Stoically, Ignatius endured the agony of a second operation, but it left him so ill with fever that it was thought he would die. He received the last sacrament and reconciled himself to death. Wracked by torturing pains, on the eve of the Feast of Saint Peter—to whom he had once written some verses—Ignatius gave himself to the care of the saint.

That night, June 27, 1521, as if in answer to the prayers, Saint Peter presented himself as Ignatius lay on his bed. That was the vision which Ignatius ever afterward claimed to have seen. Whatever the case, the crisis was turned. The next day there was a marked improvement in his condition.

Although the leg healed, it was shorter than the other, and part of the bone protruded below the knee. Nothing could be more repugnant to the vain Ignatius. Not only would he now walk with an unflattering limp, but he would not be able to wear his attractive hose and fashionable boots. Ignatius was horrified when he realized that he would be permanently disfigured.

The surgeon informed him that there was one alternative: to open the leg once more and saw off the protrusion. The thought of suffering terrible pains for a third time would have daunted most people, but not Ignatius. More concerned about his physical appearance than physical discomfort, he allowed the doctors to operate again, and for weeks he withstood harrowing treatment as his leg was placed in an iron machine to stretch it. Ignatius would one day describe that ghastly experience as the "martyrdom of vanity." Perhaps its greatest significance was that it reflected the tenacity of character which he would greatly need when he embarked on a life of holiness.

CHAPTER 2

CONVERSION AND MONTSERRAT

Ignatius was still determined to pursue his worldly aims. Indeed, that was why he had tolerated so much agony in the treatment of his leg. But meanwhile, he had to endure the tedium of convalescence. As his strength returned, he became impatient for action. With nothing to do, his boredom grew more unbearable each day.

To while away the time, Ignatius asked for a book of knightly romance. But no such book could be found in the castle. Instead, he was brought two pious works: the *Life of Our Saviour* by Ludolph of Saxony, a Carthusian monk, and *Flos sanctorum,* dealing with the lives of the saints and written in Castilian.

At first Ignatius found little to interest him in the books, but because there was no alternative he continued to read them. Confinement to a small area often compels people to do things which normally they would refuse to do.

Even so, these were not the conditions which one would expect to change a man's life so drastically. Yet that is precisely what they did. The conversion was not sudden, but as Ignatius read about the lives of Jesus and the saints, he

13

came to realize that the adventures and heroism of these people were often more courageous and exciting than any knightly career. The fact that the saints had suffered, yet accomplished so much, began to offer a challenge to him. Their achievements had needed as much—if not more—bravery as he would ever require in battle. What knight, for instance, had exceeded the undeniable courage of Saint Francis of Assisi, when he dared to try to convert the enemy sultan in Egypt? Who could match the fearlessness of Saint Paul when he opposed the might of Caesar?

The more Ignatius thought of these daring acts, inspired solely by a desire to serve God and to help one's fellowmen, the more he realized how petty his own past had been in comparison. But at times his mind would wander again to dreams of worldly distinctions. He reflected on the lovely environment and the happy moments that he had experienced both in the home of his former patron and at court. Should he return to that life and strive to attain a position of power?

These opposing thoughts set up an inner conflict that disturbed Ignatius. It persisted for some time, and then it was resolved, although no one can give the exact date of his conversion. But, gradually, introspection made him starkly conscious of the way in which he had wasted his life. Finally, he resolved to devote himself to matters of the spirit.

His first reaction was to subject himself to severe penance, then to journey barefoot, with no food except herbs, on a pilgrimage to Jerusalem. On his return he would retire to a monastery, perhaps the Carthusian house at Seville. Being the strictest of orders, the Carthusian movement par-

14

ticularly attracted him, and he instructed a servant to inquire into the Carthusians' mode of life and the details of their Rule.

Now Ignatius began to pray fervently each night. To his joy, during one of these vigils, "he saw clearly the image of Our Lady with the Holy Child, at whose sight for a notable time he felt a surpassing sweetness, which left him with such a loathing for his past sins . . . that every unclean imagination seemed blotted out from his soul. . . ." Those were the words he later wrote in his biography.

It was a time of complete conversion. If the story is accepted, the Loyola castle shook under some strange impact in that eventful moment, and a rent, which can be seen today, ran down the wall in Ignatius' room.

There are those who attribute the two mystical experiences of Ignatius to the unstable imaginings of a sick man. Yet his autobiography records that there were other occasions when he received visions of Our Lady and certain saints. By temperament, Ignatius was not prone to hallucinations, but was shrewd, practical, and strong in mind.

Now that his health was better, he was impatient to act. During February, 1522, at the age of thirty-one, he started out on the first of many eventful journeys, putting his fate implicitly in the hands of God.

Knowing that his new mode of life would sever him from his home and relatives, Ignatius left the castle without revealing his future plans. Don Martin, however, sensed that his brother was contemplating some great change, abandoning the career which their father had intended for the youngest son. As the new head of a proud family, Don Martin was anxious that Ignatius should not discredit the

15

name of Loyola. But he did not propose to interfere with Ignatius' plans, whatever they might be.

In a worldly and materialistic sense, Don Martin was right in believing that Ignatius was casting away a life that promised rich rewards. Spain had entered upon a golden age. For seven centuries the Spaniards had suffered the humiliation of Moors on their soil, but now the Muslims had fled forever from the fury of Spanish arms. Successfully fighting France for the possession of southern Italy, Spain had included the kingdom of Naples among its dominions. This war held special significance for Ignatius, for two of his brothers died in battle. The struggle for the mastery of Italy persisted.

A third brother had also died, but under far more adventurous circumstances. He had been among those Spaniards who had ventured into the Atlantic Ocean to gaze on the New World.

Ignatius had been born into an age of great endeavor and conquest. Men were seeking change, and trying to break out from what had long been a limited world. They were stimulated by a sense of discovery and adventure. There was an inquiring spirit in learning. People were affected by the sharp impact of movements such as the Renaissance and the Reformation. Feudalism had yielded to the birth of city-states. In Europe, monarchies were gathering enormous power, jockeying for mastery, and trying to found new empires. Spanish power was penetrating into Europe and beyond the seas. As if to fix a seal to Spanish might, the young King Charles would be elected emperor of the Holy Roman Empire, and his regent, Ximénes, would be appointed as pope.

16

In all these circumstances, a military career, backed by influence, offered tremendous scope and opportunities. But Ignatius would not abandon his newly found ideals. To give no hint of his intentions, he explained to his brother that he must, out of courtesy, report to his former commander, the Duke of Nájera. He said to Don Martin: "Sir, as you know, the duke of Nájera is aware that I am well again. It will be no more than my duty for me to go to Navarrete where he is."

Thus, Ignatius went out into the world, having no idea of the pattern of his future beyond that in some way he would serve God. In his possession was a book of some three hundred pages bound in vermilion, gold, and blue. It contained the holy thoughts that had occurred to him during convalescence. He would take it with him always.

Accompanied by another brother and two servants, Ignatius first traveled to Onate to the home of a married sister. On the way he prayed at the shrine of Our Lady of Aranzazu, returning, as one writer has said, "the visit which his heavenly Mistress had paid him."

Bidding his brother good-bye, Ignatius went on to Navarrete where the duke was surprised to learn that the former soldier proposed to leave his service. Ignatius received some ducats that were owed him. He used them to repay certain debts, and what remained was given toward repairing a dilapidated figure of Our Lady. Having discharged his obligations, there was no need to stay at Navarrete longer. So, after some days, Ignatius told his servants to return to Loyola, while he set off for Catalonia. There he intended to do penance at the Church of Our Lady of Montserrat, which,

17

along with a celebrated Benedictine monastery, stands high upon one of the bulky Pyrenean heights.

At some point on this journey after he had left Cervera, a town some fifty miles west of Barcelona, Ignatius met a Moor who also rode a mule. After learning of Ignatius' destination, the stranger began an argument by scoffing at the Virgin Mary. For a while the exchanges were heated, until the Moor, hastening his mount, went on ahead.

Ignatius was so incensed that, for a time, he was tempted to hurry after the Moor and kill him. The infidel had told him where he would leave the highway and follow a track to a certain village. But as Ignatius approached the fork in the road, he could not make up his mind what to do. Finally, and rather naïvely, he dropped the rein on the mule's neck; he would let the animal decide. If it chose the path, Ignatius would kill the Moor. If it followed the road the Moor would live. Not unnaturally, the beast kept to the easier highway, sparing the Moor's life.

Ignatius' colorful mantle, hose, and feathered cap were unsuited to a person committed to poverty, so when he reached a little mountain town, he bought sackcloth (which he had made into a gown), a piece of rope to fasten around his waist, hempen shoes (although he is said to have discarded the right one because his wounded leg and foot were still swollen), and a pilgrim's staff with water gourd.

Thus equipped, Ignatius arrived at Montserrat in the Pyrenees. This gargantuan hodgepodge of pinnacles and crazy shapes resembles the teeth of a saw. The highest peak soars from the plain to some twelve thousand feet, and roughly two-thirds of the way up its craggy sides stand the shrine of Our Lady and the Benedictine abbey.

At that time, the abbey was reached only with difficulty. An old account says: "It is a stupendous monastery, built on the top of a huge landrock, whither it is impossible to go up, or come down by a direct way, but a path is cut out full of Windings and Turnings; and on the Crown of this Craggy hill there is a flat, upon which the Monastery and Pilgrimage place is founded, where there is a picture of the Virgin Mary, sunburnt and tann'd, it seems, when she went to Egypt."

Just as it is today, Montserrat had long been a mecca for European pilgrims. When Ignatius arrived, the abbey was home to seventy monks, ninety lay brothers, and a choir of thirty young men, called "Our Lady's Boys." Higher up beyond the monastery were thirteen cells named after various saints. Each was occupied by a hermit, whose austere life was dedicated entirely to prayer. The hermit occupying the cell of Saint Benedict was the superior over the rest.

One of the monks at that time was widely known for his sanctity. He was the hermit of Saint Damas, Father Jean Chanones. A Frenchman who had been vicar-general of Mirepoix at the age of thirty-two, Chanones had made a pilgrimage to Montserrat and had decided to quit the world for a life of prayer. He was the person whom Ignatius now sought. For three days the young man wrote a confession of his sins, anxious not to omit any detail, and vowing perpetual chastity. Ignatius not only exposed his past to Chanones, but he asked for counsel for the future. There is no record of what the monk advised.

19

Finally, Ignatius was given absolution, but there was one more thing to do. Years earlier—in his days of vanity, as he described them—he had been impressed by *Amadis of Gaul*, a popular book that described how cavaliers, on being received into an order of chivalry, fulfilled the vigil of the armor. Briefly, before embarking on adventure, they prayed throughout the night before the altar of the Virgin Mary.

Ignatius, too, was to don new armor—the pilgrim's humble dress in which he would accomplish immortal deeds as a soldier of Christ. So, on March 24, 1522, on the eve of the Annunciation, he gave his nobleman's clothes to a beggar. Wearing sackcloth, he entered the Church of Our Lady. There he hung up his sword and dagger, and spent the night in lonely vigil.

CHAPTER 3

MANRESA

In the morning of March 25, 1522, Ignatius heard Mass and received Holy Communion. Then he set off along a mountain track that led to the small town of Manresa. Wishing to be completely poor, he had left his mule at Montserrat. Walking, however, imposed a strain, for he still moved with a limp. While he was resting by the wayside about noon, four women and two youths came along the road. Ignatius asked if they could tell him where he could lodge for the night.

One of the women, who was older than the rest, gave her name as Iñes Pascual. She lived in Barcelona, but was staying in Manresa where she owned property. As it was a feast day, she and her friends had attended Mass at Montserrat and were now going back to Manresa.

Ignatius gladly accepted her invitation to travel with them. He puzzled his new companions, for despite his poverty-stricken appearance he spoke in the manner of a gentleman. Yet he would not disclose any details about himself. They were even more curious when a monk, hurrying up to them on horseback, asked Ignatius if he was the person

21

who had given his fine clothes to a beggar the day before. Accused of having stolen the clothes, the poor fellow had been arrested despite his plea of innocence. The man, Ignatius assured the monk, had spoken the truth, but he said nothing more. He merely reproached himself, saying: "Ah, sinner that thou art, thou couldst not even do thy neighbour a service without causing him an injury."

At Manresa, Doña Pascual, who was to become a lifelong friend, obtained a room for Ignatius at a hostel, the Hospital of Saint Lucy. She also arranged to send him food daily. However, Ignatius usually gave it away to the sick and the poor, confining his own diet to black bread and water. Only on Sundays did he allow himself to take wine and herbs, and even then the herbs were mixed with ashes. The slightest hint of luxury was forbidden. Indeed, he seemed determined to punish himself relentlessly for past sins. He even endured the discomfort of a hair shirt, and girdled his waist with a chain or a belt woven from prickly leaves. At nights he slept on the floor, using a piece of wood or a stone for a pillow.

Under these austerities the young man's appearance very quickly deteriorated. His red hair and beard grew long and unkempt, and his nails were uncut and dirty. Indeed, his degeneracy even roused the contempt of beggars, and children scoffed, calling him "Father Sack."

Ignatius attended Mass and Vespers each day, and on occasion served at the altar. He also devoted seven hours daily to prayer, pleading with God for guidance. Sometimes he stayed at a local Dominican monastery where the monks allowed him the use of a cell. He frequently read the story of the Passion of Christ, and derived a certain measure of peace from it. He also helped to tend the sick in the hospital, yet once the sight of sores and disease affected him so profoundly that he forced himself to embrace the patients to suppress his revulsion.

There is little doubt that Ignatius' asceticism was inspired by what he had read of the early saints. Yet at times even the cell at the Dominican monastery did not give him the solitude he craved. When in such a mood he would retire to a cave on the other side of the Cardoner River. Some twenty feet long and about six feet wide, the cave—today a famous grotto—was concealed by bushes.

During his stay at Manresa, Ignatius knew moments of extreme ecstasy, but more often than not—doubtless caused by such harsh privations—he was reduced to a state of deep depression. This greatly disturbed him, for he was still tormented by the memory of former sins. He remembered when he and others had plundered an orchard. They had concealed their guilt, and an innocent man of Azpeitia had been imprisoned.

To his dismay, Ignatius was often the victim of temptations. Moreover, he felt that his devotion to God was less profound than it should be. In this state of mental confusion, he would seek the solitude of the cave. But even there he could not always rid himself of agonizing doubts. Tormenting him was the fear that he had failed to disclose all his sins at Montserrat.

In his despair, Ignatius even doubted the merit of prayer, and his doubt left him with an emptiness of the soul. Frequently, he would plead for God's mercy in the words of Saint Paul: "O wretched man that I am! Who shall deliver me from the body of this death?"

23

Once he prayed for a whole week in the chapel of Our Lady of Villadordid, not far from Manresa. He was so seriously affected by doubts that he questioned if he could really endure the life he had planned for himself. This query deeply troubled him, adding to his mental turmoil and the despondency that had fallen upon him.

More mortifications, Ignatius thought, would surely achieve the peace and tranquillity he sought. So, he began to abstain more and more from eating.

His enforced penances—especially the fasting—were so exacting that his body suffered under the strain. He was found in the chapel of Villadordid after he had collapsed, so exhausted that it was necessary to carry him to the Dominican monastery. Even then he stubbornly insisted on continuing his abstinence. Only when his confessor threatened to refuse him absolution did he end his fast.

Once, having prayed in the church of Saint Paul on the outskirts of the town, Ignatius sat in meditation beside the Cardoner River. "Suddenly there fell upon his soul an illumination of supernatural light." In that moment, as he was to claim for the rest of his life, supernatural things were exposed to him. He said that in a vision God revealed to him the future Society of Jesus. Years later, whenever he was asked about the constitution of his movement, Ignatius would reply: "I saw it thus at Manresa."

After that revelation, as he subsequently explained, Ignatius cast himself down before a nearby crucifix. He observed an apparition about the cross that he had seen once before at the Hospital of Saint Lucy, and was to see at other times afterward. It took the form of a luminous snake with eyes of fire, and Ignatius accepted it as a vision from the devil.

In Manresa, Ignatius also saw apparitions of Christ and the Blessed Virgin. In later years, he told how he saw the vision of Our Lady on twenty to forty occasions—"always by an interior perception and without sensible distinction of the corporeal members." He further asserted that while he stood on the steps of the Dominican church, God, in yet another vision, gave him an insight into the mystery of the Trinity. Once, he lay as though dead for an entire week, although the doctors noted that his heart beat regularly. When he came to, he merely remarked: "O Jesus! Jesus!" Never did he describe to anyone what had happened during those mysterious days.

Ignatius was one of the most practical of all those who became saints; at the same time he was one of the most mystical. For the rest of his life supernatural sights would come to him, and there is little doubt that they helped to mold his spiritual outlook. Originally, Ignatius had intended to spend a short while at Manresa. Instead, he stayed there for almost a year, perhaps the most significant period of his life. It had been a spiritual battleground in which he later said he had overcome the devil's temptations. He had won the victory of his own soul, enabling him in the days to come to direct others in the salvation of souls.

His experiences were recorded in his now famous book under the title *Spiritual Exercises*. The book described the ways in which he had warded off temptation, and the Exercises were so arranged that when they eventually came to be used by others, they could be carried out under the guid-

25

ance of a spiritual director. The object of the Exercises was to assist anyone who wished to be brought closer to God. At first the rules were to have been simple, but as he dwelt more on his experiences at Manresa the Exercises grew far more complex.

Because he had often prayed at midnight, Ignatius decided that the Exercises should start at that hour. They should next be made on waking in the morning. Before or after Mass would be the occasion for the third stage, and the fourth would occur in the evening at the time of Vespers.

The Spiritual Exercises were split up into four weeks, the first devoted to repentance. During the other weeks, the devotee concentrated on the contemplation of Jesus Christ, and on His life and its meaning. Ignatius stressed the need to reflect the Lord's sufferings and to strive to emulate Him. He drew attention to the way in which Christ had preferred poverty to wealth, had symbolized humility as opposed to vanity, and had humbly borne contempt.

Ignatius asserted that there were three categories of humility, of which he wrote: "The first lies in this, that I go humbly obedient to the law of God in all things, and not violate any commandment, whether of God or His Vicar, that binds me under pain of mortal sin. The second lies in this, that I am indifferent to riches, honour and health, and that I would not bring upon myself the pain of venial sin. And the third, which is the most perfect humility, lies in this, that I desire poverty and contempt and the lowliness of fools and to be treated as Christ was treated before me."

This unusual man, who had now discovered his mission in life amid the peace and quiet of the Manresa cave, also wrote: "The more that the soul is alone and apart from others, the more fit it becomes to draw near to its Creator and to be united with Him; and the more intimately it is united with Him, the more likely is it to receive the holy grace of its Creator."

The *Spiritual Exercises*, amended and amplified at various times in later years, were to become one of the main authoritative formularies of his Order. They would influence millions more, both laymen and clergy. To a large extent, this little manual of discipline was to be to the Society of Jesus what the Rule is to the older religious Orders. Ignatius eventually used the *Spiritual Exercises* to give spiritual retreats to others, especially his followers.

The day was approaching when Ignatius would leave Manresa. He was already aware, although he still did not know the details, that God had ordained that he should found a religious movement to serve Christ. However, disciples of the caliber required for such an Order were not to be found in Manresa. There, some resented his begging and his brand of piety. Consequently, they mocked and derided him. Yet others—particularly some of the wealthier women—chose to follow his example. They received the sacraments so regularly that the more worldly nicknamed them "las Iñiguas."

These pious people, and the ones like Doña Pascual who had befriended him, were abused and often attacked. Even so, this did not deter them from helping their revered recluse. When, for instance, Ignatius fell seriously ill toward the end of 1522, they took him to the house of a man named Andres Amigant, and later to the home of a man named Ferreira.

Friends finally prevailed on Ignatius to take greater care of his health and appearance. To protect him from the weather, a wool manufacturer called Canielles gave him two short cloaks of a coarse gray cloth and a cap of the same material.

The year's penance that Ignatius had set himself upon leaving the castle of Loyola was completed. He was now about thirty-two years old, and he would go on his pilgrimage to Jerusalem. This would entail sailing from Barcelona to Gaeta in the kingdom of Naples. From there he would journey to Rome to secure his pilgrim's license from the pope. Then he would go to Venice, Cyprus, and finally the Holy Land. The voyage would be hazardous, for hostile Turkish ships controlled much of the Mediterranean waters.

Barcelona, some thirty miles away, had been ravaged by the plague. When the port was again free, Ignatius left Manresa in February, 1523, in the company of Canon Antonio Pujol, the brother of Doña Pascual and confessor to the archbishop of Tarragona.

CHAPTER 4

PILGRIMAGE TO JERUSALEM

Ignatius now took greater care of himself. He had been given a pair of tough boots, but possessed no stockings, and he wore a jerkin and breeches, as well as the gray wool tunic. What he lacked was money, but Providence, he believed, would solve all the financial difficulties that would arise.

Unable to get immediate passage to Italy, he spent his time in Barcelona attending church, visiting the sick, and talking to the local monks and hermits.

While listening to a Lenten sermon in the Church of Santa Maria del Mar, Ignatius, who was sitting on the altar steps, was noticed by a pious lady, the wife of an affluent but blind nobleman. Doña Isabel Roser had an almost irresistible desire to speak to Ignatius. She said that his head seemed to be encircled with light.

Doña Roser told her husband of her strange experience, and he advised her to find the stranger and extend their hospitality to him. During a meal on the following day, Ignatius told his hosts of his intentions. The Rosers tried to induce him to stay in Barcelona, but he refused. Yet, in response to Doña Isabel's plea, he agreed not to sail in a certain brigantine. This was fortunate, for the vessel went down with all on board.

It was arranged that Ignatius should be a passenger in a safer ship which would also carry the bishop of Barcelona, a kinsman of Doña Isabel's husband. The captain consented to a free passage if Ignatius supplied his own food. Doña Isabel offered him the necessary provisions, but he insisted on begging for his food in the streets. Wishing to embark in abject poverty, he placed several coins on a stone bench before he boarded the ship. Whoever found the coins could keep them.

Arriving in Gaeta, after a five-day journey, Ignatius trekked along the Appian Way to Rome. With him were three other pilgrims—a young man, and a mother and her daughter. All four begged for their food.

The journey was quite eventful, for the plague was spreading terror in central Italy. Ignatius, his face haggard due to privations, was often thought to be carrying disease. People shrank away when he asked for alms.

The pilgrims stayed at a farm the first night, and although the women were admitted to the house, Ignatius and the young man had to sleep in the stable. About midnight he was awakened by the women's cries; they were being assaulted. When he rushed to their aid, the assailants took flight. Ignatius and his companions then thought it better to continue their journey even in the darkness. When they reached the next town, they found the gate locked and so they retired to a church. Due to the epidemic, they were refused admission to the town in the morning.

The little party decided to travel on, but Ignatius was too

weary to accompany them. It was his good fortune that a lady with influence had him admitted to the town, where he rested for two days.

Ignatius arrived in Rome on Palm Sunday, 1523. With other pilgrims he received his license and blessing from Pope Adrian VI. However, he did not leave the city at once, for people warned him that without money there was little chance of reaching the Holy Land. His begging yielded a number of ducats, but when he eventually set off for Venice he reproved himself for not trusting God to provide for his needs, and so he gave his money to the poor.

Wherever he went, Ignatius—and his fellow travelers— were shunned by the people. The plague still raged on, and strangers were unpopular. Travelers spent many nights in the open. On reaching Chioggia, the pilgrims heard that they could not enter Venice without a certificate proving that they were free from infection. They were told that doctors would examine them at Padua.

Ignatius was too exhausted once again to keep pace with his companions, and they went on without him. But that night, as he slept, Christ—so Ignatius related—consoled him in a vision. Nothing, the Lord said, would prevent him from entering Venice. One story describes how city officials closely scrutinized the papers of other pilgrims, but ignored Ignatius. Another account, however, related that the quarantine regulations were relaxed on the day that Ignatius reached the city.

Yet problems still beset him. He had given away his ducats, and, unable to speak Italian, he had difficulty in begging or seeking lodgings. Consequently, he decided to spend his first night sleeping in the arcade of the Procura-

31

tori in the Piazza of Saint Mark. While he lay on the hard pavement, a rich and pious senator, Marc Antoni Trevisani, a future doge (chief magistrate) of Venice, was roused from slumber by a voice that said, "What! Sleepest thou in thy bed, when My poor servant lies so near on the bare stone?"

Sending for servants and lanterns, Trevisani searched for Ignatius, and took him home. However, Ignatius would stay only for one night; to remain longer was contrary to his ideal of poverty. Indeed, his main concern was to secure a passage to Jaffa. But this was both difficult and dangerous. There was the risk of capture at sea, for the Turks now occupied the island of Rhodes.

Days merged into weeks. Lack of adequate food undermined Ignatius' health, and he became ill again. The turning point in his fortunes came with a chance encounter; he met Simón Contez, a wealthy merchant from Ignatius' own province in Spain. The Biscayan promptly asked Ignatius to be his guest. More important to Ignatius, Contez arranged an interview with Andrea Gritti, the elderly doge. Gritti listened patiently to Ignatius' plea for a free passage on the admiral's ship, which was to take the lieutenant governor to Cyprus.

The courteous doge granted the request, but doctors warned that if Ignatius made the voyage his illness would most likely prove fatal. Yet nothing could deter him. To all the arguments urging him to end his pilgrimage, Ignatius simply replied: "I have such confidence in God, Our Saviour, that, if this year one ship or plank of wood were to cross to Jerusalem, I would go with it."

On July 14, 1523, the ship set sail. Curiously, after a bout of seasickness, Ignatius felt much better. Soon he was rousing the hostility of the crew by scolding them for lewd behavior. They plotted to abandon him on a lonely island, but the wind blew with such force that the vessel had to go on to Cyprus. There, it went no farther. Fortunately, however, *The Pilgrim*—so named because it carried pilgrims from Venice to the East—was still in Salamis harbor. Ignatius joined the ship after a walk of some five miles, and, on the last day of August, he landed at Jaffa, the port for Jerusalem. Ignatius had achieved his ambition; he had set foot in the Holy Land.

The pilgrims continued their journey on mules. When they approached Jerusalem they were met by Franciscan fathers carrying a cross. Dismounting, they entered the Holy City.

So far, God had given Ignatius no idea where he should found his company of Jesus. As he knelt and meditated at the sacred places where Jesus had suffered the agony and passion, Ignatius fervently hoped that the Lord would indicate that he should remain in Jerusalem and try to convert the infidels.

What seems incredible is that Ignatius believed he could convert the Turks either single-handed or at best with a comparatively meager following. Believing that Muhammadanism was the greatest foe of the Roman Catholic Church, he appears to have been unaware of, or indifferent to, the growing threat of Lutheranism inside the Church itself. On the other hand, it is not known if he regarded the situation from political and military standpoints. The menace of the Turks was increasing. Having occupied Egypt, Syria, and Belgrade, they would advance almost into Vienna.

In attempting to convert the Turks, Ignatius intended to rely not on force but on persuasion and preaching, a method he would always employ when he founded his Order. But he does not seem to have been fully conscious of the situation that existed in Jerusalem. The Franciscan Order was the custodian of the Holy Places, and there could be no innovation without the consent of the Father Provincial. This dignitary was then in Bethlehem, but on his return at the end of October, Ignatius spoke to him, saying that he wished to stay in Jerusalem to create a society that would prove that the battle was not between Christian and Muslim, but for the mastery of the soul within everyone.

The Provincial admired Ignatius for his courage and zeal but he could not, he explained, allow him to remain. He doubted if Ignatius, because of his temperament, could comply with local conditions. It was almost inevitable, said the Provincial, that Ignatius would antagonize the Turks, who had agreed to guarantee rights of pilgrimage only if the pilgrims did not violate the rules. Any pilgrim who strayed from the prescribed bounds could be seized by the Turks, and even executed or sold into slavery. Indeed, sometimes the Turks ransomed some of their victims, but the Franciscans had little money for that purpose. The Provincial explained with gentle firmness that anyone who infringed those rules might jeopardize the whole Christian community. As the head of Christians in the Holy Land, he could not take that risk.

34

Stubbornly, Ignatius said that he had resolved to stay if by so doing he would not offend God. The Provincial replied that disobedience would certainly offend God, and that he was empowered by the Holy See to excommunicate anyone who did not do as he was told. Ignatius submitted and prepared to depart with the other pilgrims.

But before he left, Ignatius committed an act that might have endangered all the Catholics in Jerusalem. Despite what the Provincial had told him, he decided to visit the Mount of Olives, and he went with neither Turkish guard nor guide. He wished to see the impressions that tradition claims were the footprints of Christ before He ascended into heaven.

Bribing the guard with a penknife, Ignatius hurried to the hallowed spot. He knelt there for a while, but on the way back he suddenly wanted to know in which direction the footprints pointed. This time he bribed the guard with a pair of scissors.

But his infringement of the rules was not to go unnoticed. On descending the mount once more, he encountered an Armenian servant of the Franciscans. As the man bustled him back to the monks, Ignatius, as he would one day reveal, beheld a vision of Christ in the air, and it assuaged the sharp rebuke that awaited him at the monastery.

When Ignatius and his fellow pilgrims reached Cyprus, he begged for a free passage in a large ship. Someone told the captain that Ignatius was a saint, whereupon the skipper suggested that if such were the case, he should walk on the waters.

But the master of a smaller, decrepit vessel was much more charitable. The two ships, and a Turkish one, left harbor the same day, two of them to disaster. In the evening, during a terrible storm, the Turkish ship sank with all hands. And although no one was drowned, the larger of the remaining ships was wrecked on the coast of Cyprus. Only the little vessel survived.

Ignatius arrived in Venice during January, 1524. It had been a tedious voyage lasting two and a half months, but in that time he reached an important decision. He had been bewildered after he was prevented from founding his company of disciples in Jerusalem. Consequently, he had turned to the Bible. While reading the Gospel, the words "they understood none of these things" made him stop and think. He had been a courtier, yet, he now realized, he was actually unlettered. In preparing himself for a military career, he had neglected matters of the intellect.

As he read the Scriptures, it occurred to him that he could never properly lead others to God if he failed to combine love of God with sound reasoning. The thought worried him, and with characteristic determination he resolved to put the matter right. He would return to Spain and study as if he were a child once more.

Ignatius did not remain long in Venice. It is believed that he left in February. This time he had money, perhaps the gift of Simón Contez, the Biscayan merchant. Ignatius set off on foot to Genoa, a journey fraught with danger due to the war then raging in northern Italy between Spain and France.

Once again he failed to keep his scanty riches. In the cathedral at Ferrara he distributed his money to beggars, who, because of his generosity, loudly hailed him as a saint. Completely poor once more, he continued his journey.

By choosing a particular route he attempted to evade the conflicting forces. Yet he was captured by a Spanish patrol who suspected him of espionage. However, when he was questioned by an officer his replies were so naïve that the captors were reprimanded for not knowing the difference between a fool and a spy.

Next, Ignatius was taken prisoner by the French, but the interrogating officer happened to be a Basque Frenchman, who courteously offered him supper.

Fortune favored him again at Genoa, for there he was recognized by someone he had known at the court of Ferdinand and Isabella. Don Rodrigo Portuodo arranged a passage for him to Spain. Although Portuodo's flotilla was chased by the enemy, it reached Barcelona during the end of February or early in March, 1524. Ignatius had been absent from Spain for almost a year.

CHAPTER 5

"THE PEOPLE IN SACKS"

Ignatius quickly renewed his friendship with Isabel Roser, who not only encouraged him to study, but was willing to engage a tutor named Geronimo Ardebalo. However, Ignatius declined the offer, preferring, instead, an aged Cistercian whom he had met at Manresa. But when he traveled to see the old man, Ignatius learned that he had died.

Returning to Barcelona, Ignatius decided that a tutor was unsuitable for him at that stage. So he attended a local school to learn Latin and grammar. A man in his thirties, sitting in a class of boys, was an incongruous sight, yet it also demonstrated Ignatius' sense of discipline.

For a while he had the use of a room in the house of Iñes Pascual, and she asked her brother, Father Pujol, to lend him books.

But Ignatius was eventually to realize that he had made a wrong decision. Whatever the cause, he was slow to learn, a fact that amused his fellow pupils. At the end of two years he had to admit that he had learned very little. After wasting so much time, he now consented to study with Master Ardebalo. In the Church of Santa Maria del Mar, he told

39

his new teacher that he had been inattentive at times in school. He had devoted, for instance, many hours to prayer when he should have been in the classroom, and sometimes he had visited the sick.

He pleaded with Ardebalo to beat him, in the way that he would beat other pupils, if he should again yield to distractions. No one can say if Ardebalo ever thrashed him, but it is known that Ignatius—from the time that he first left Manresa—often flogged himself as a penance. And as part of his self-discipline, he persisted in sleeping on the floor.

He was now more attentive to his clothes, presenting a clerical appearance by donning a black cassock. Beneath was the hair shirt. He also wore shoes, but apparently the soles were missing as a further mortification. Ignatius continued to beg for food, but usually gave most of it to the poor—sometimes to the workers and children in the Pascual house, part of which was a cotton factory.

Iñes' son Juan revered Ignatius, and on oath he once claimed that while peering into Ignatius' room through a chink in the door, he saw him rise more than two feet in the air while in prayer. Years later Juan would tell his family: "If you had known that guest of ours, so holy and so gentle, you would never tire of kissing the ground which his feet had touched."

As at Manresa, Ignatius inspired both admiration and hate. He was insulted in the streets, and even the servants in the Pascual home were offensive. But Ignatius accepted all the abuse with calm and dignity, and he even pleaded with Iñes Pascual not to punish her servants. However, the enmity that he roused almost led to his death. Just outside the city—not far from the San Daniel gate—stood a Dominican nunnery, the Convent of the Angels. Corruption was rather rife among the nuns, who were in the habit of seeing certain dissolute young men. When Ignatius protested to the nuns, they were so impressed by his sincerity that they adhered once again to the tenets of their Rule.

This so annoyed the young men that they hired two Moors to attack Ignatius. On occasions Father Pujol accompanied him, and one day, as they left the convent, they were set upon so fiercely that Pujol died from his injuries. For a while it appeared that Ignatius would also die. A kindhearted miller had placed him on his mule and taken him home, where he lay close to death for thirty days. On the last day it seemed so certain that he would not recover that he received the final sacrament.

No one could induce Ignatius to expose the ones guilty of the crime. After two months, when he could walk again, he ignored his friend's advice and returned to the convent. As he was leaving, a merchant named Ribeira admitted that he had instigated the assault, and he sought Ignatius' forgiveness, which was readily given.

Of all the people he had met since he had left his ancestral home, there was no one whom Ignatius considered suitable as a disciple. Therefore, he had no followers. But this was to change in Barcelona. He now selected three young men: Calixto Saa of Segovia, Juan de Arteaga y Evendano of Estepa, and Diego Caeres, also of Segovia and a member of the court of the Viceroy of Catalonia. In one sense, however, these men cannot be regarded as the pioneer members of the Jesuit movement, for none persisted in imitating Ignatius' way of life.

Ignatius also rejected two other candidates. To Miguel Rodis, he prophesied: "You will not follow me, but one day a son of yours will enter the religious order which by God's grace I shall found." This prediction would prove correct. The second candidate was Juan Pascual, to whom he remarked: "You will marry a woman of great virtue and will have many sons and daughters; and on their account you will have many sorrows and misfortunes, which will be sent to you by God out of love for you and with remission of your sins." This, too, would prove correct. Juan's oldest son was born deaf and without speech, and the second went insane. The third led a debauched life and died at his father's feet. Finally, whatever means Juan possessed vanished as marriage portions for his daughters. He was reduced to extreme poverty, but, as Ignatius had predicted, he found happiness in that humble status.

Two years had gone by since Ignatius had started his studies, and Ardebalo told him that he should now enter a university. Ignatius proved that he had attained the necessary standard of competence by passing the examinations supervised by theologians.

In August, 1526, at the age of about thirty-five, Ignatius went to the university at Alcalá de Henares. This seat of learning had been founded by Cardinal Ximénes, who had risen from the humble status of friar and parish priest to eminence as the regent of Spain. The university had achieved fame in Europe by publishing a polyglot Bible, so named because Hebrew, Greek, and Latin versions were printed in neighboring columns. Ignatius probably chose Alcalá because Ximénes had generously donated money to assist poor scholars. His three disciples went with him.

In Alcalá, Ignatius discovered that he had arrived too early; the term did not begin until St. Luke's Day, October 18. He decided against residing at one of the students' inns, and instead went to work at the Hospital of Antecana. There he accepted his fourth follower. One of the patients, a fifteen-year-old French page of the Viceroy of Navarre, persuaded Ignatius to let him join his little company. Named Jean, he was dubbed Juanico because of his youth.

The party of five dressed alike in gray sackcloth, and they were nicknamed "the people in sacks."

Although Ignatius was essentially a man of peace, he somehow could not avoid making enemies. One day, after preaching to patients in the hospital, he was approached by a priest who asked him on whose authority he interpreted Catholic doctrine. Ignatius had just explained to his listeners the difference between mortal and venial sins, and the priest suggested that such matters should be confined to people specially ordained for that purpose.

Ignatius denied that he was a heretic. Yet it was obvious from the priest's manner that he was under suspicion.

Heresy was not uncommon in Spain, although perhaps it did not exist to the same extent as in certain other countries. The questioning, however, gave Ignatius some concern. But this was not the only thing that worried him. Of late he had noticed that more people were becoming unfriendly. Some questioned his motives as they saw him and his followers working among the poor. Others thought that he was trying to introduce reforms that were contrary to accepted Catholic doctrine.

Perhaps these suspicions arose because of Ignatius' ability to influence and lead others. He was now catechiz-

43

ing in the streets, and to his delight was giving the Spiritual Exercises. Frequently, he addressed groups of people both in the hospital and at the university. Sooner or later something must happen, but what would be the outcome?

Ignatius was living in the house of the hospital warden. One night, awakened by his host, he was told that two strangers wished to speak with him. It was clear from the warden's anxious manner that something was wrong. Very soon Ignatius learned that he was under arrest by the Inquisition.

Sanctioned by the pope, the Inquisition was a court of inquiry that mercilessly rooted out heretics. In every Catholic country, with the exception of Spain, it was supervised by the bishops. In Spain, it had been set up by King Ferdinand in 1480, with the approval of Pope Sixtus IV.

Inquisitors generally were priests, but some laymen—accomplished in interrogation—were also appointed. The courts themselves were conducted in all the leading centers under the direction of each respective diocese.

No inquisition was held at Alcalá because the city was in the archdiocese of Toledo. Therefore, until an inquisitor arrived to question him, Ignatius was committed to a cell in the local jail. Thus, for some days he had time to reflect on his activities in Alcalá.

Doubtless he had earned the annoyance of some people because of his unorthodox ideas. For instance, in Ignatius' day it was customary for Catholics not to take the sacraments very often. In official quarters it was believed that to take part in the sacraments too frequently would lead to excessive familiarity and irreverence. Indeed, a Dr. Alonso Sanchez of the Church of San Justo had even refused Communion to one of Ignatius' admirers. The person concerned had intended to take it on the octave of a feast, in addition to the feast.

Ignatius had been encouraging people to participate in the sacraments every Sunday and on all feast days. Therefore, one cannot condemn the Inquisition for wishing to know more about the man whose magnetism was inducing people to do what the Church discouraged.

The visiting examiner was Miguel Carrasco, a canon of San Justo, and he was assisted by Alonso de Mexia. Ignatius stood before them on November 19, 1526. It is interesting to read an extract from the official record of the inquiry because it affords an insight into Ignatius' way of evangelical teaching and style of living at this period. It says:

> In the city of Alcalá de Henares, on the 19th day of November, 1526, before Dr. Miguel Carrasco, a canon of Santa Justa in the said city, the licentiate Alonso de Mexia, canon of Toledo, and before me, Francisco Ximénes, notary: Fray Hernando Rubio, presbyter, of the Order of St. Francis, forty-one years of age, being duly sworn, and asked what he knew concerning certain young men who go about the city, clad in light grey smocks that reach to the feet, some of them barefoot, and say that they live after the manner of the apostles, said—
>
> That what he knew was this: He had seen now and again in the city, four or five such men clad as described, one or two of them went barefoot. And once, about two months before, the witness had started off

45

in company with a boy to fetch a peck of flour that he wanted, and had gone to the house of Isabel, the bedeswoman who lived behind the Church of St. Francis; when he got there he opened the door, and saw in the court, carpeted by a grass matting, one of the aforesaid, who went barefoot, a young man, perhaps twenty years old. Two or three women were kneeling round him, their hands folded as if in prayer, and looking at the young man, who was talking. The witness did not hear what was said. One of the women was the said bedeswoman, who exclaimed, when she saw the witness, "Leave us alone, Padre, as we are busy." And that same day, in the afternoon, the bedeswoman came to the witness and said: "Padre, don't be shocked by what you saw today; that man is a saint."

When asked if he knew whether these young men had held other meetings, he answered that he had heard say that they met at a certain hour of the day in the hospice of Our Lady . . . that the young men spoke there, and men and women went to hear them.

Asked if the young men lived together, he said no, each lived alone . . . he did not know whether they were new Christians [that is, persons descended from Jewish ancestry within four generations] or old Christians [persons of pure Christian ancestry].

Beatriz Ramires . . . said that once she was at the house of Andres Davila, a baker, and there in a room was the said Iñigo and one of his companions. Various persons were listening to Iñigo. Isabel Sanchez . . . and del Vado, housekeeper for Fray Bernardino, the daughter of Juana de Villarejo, a girl of about

fourteen, the said Andres Davila, and his wife, and
also the wife of Francisco de la Morenna, and another
man, a vine-dresser; she thought there were others as
well but she did not remember who. Iñigo was instructing them in the two great commandments, that
is, Thou shalt love God, etc., etc.; he spoke at great
length on this subject; and the witness was vexed to
find that while she was there Iñigo said nothing that
was new to her, merely all about loving God and your
neighbour.

. . . Caceres and Arteaga shared a room in the
house of Hernando de Parra, Calixto and Juanico de
Reinalde lived with Andres Davila, and Iñigo lived in
the hospital of Antejana, and she had seen some of
them together in Iñigo's room. They were all young
men. Sometimes they received some little presents, a
bunch of grapes, a slice of ham, etc., in return for
their teachings, but the presents were thrust upon
them, against their will. She herself had persuaded
some rich ladies to give Iñigo the cloth for the gar-
ment he wore. A mattress also and two coverlets were
given, and one mattress lent, and she had given a pillow stuffed with wool to Calixto and Joannes.

The Inquisitors wished to learn if Ignatius and his small
band were part of a sect that had tried to spread heresy in
Seville. They asked him many questions and also examined others, including the people with whom he lodged.
But in the end they could find nothing wrong with Ignatius' teachings or attitude toward the Church. Before
returning to Toledo they instructed Juan Rodriguez de

47

Figueroa, grand vicar to the archbishop of Toledo, to continue the questioning.

Figueroa arrived at the same conclusion as had Carrasco and de Mexia. He merely ordered Ignatius and his companions not to dress in a similar manner since they were not a religious Order. Their hoods must vary in color. There was also a later suggestion that they should wear shoes.

CHAPTER 6

FROM ALCALA TO SALAMANCA

If Ignatius thought that he had seen the last of the Inquisition, he was to be disappointed. Several months later he was again in trouble. He had been to Segovia, where his disciple Calixto had been taken ill. No sooner was he back in Alcalá than he was arrested, although no charge was disclosed. He was taken to the clerics' prison.

On their way to jail, Ignatius and his escort were compelled to stand aside in a narrow street to allow a colorful procession to go by. The central figure was Francis Borgia, Marquis de Lomby, the seventeen-year-old son of the duke of Gandia. He was proceeding from the palace of his uncle, the archbishop of Saragossa, to the court of the Emperor Charles V at Valladolid.

It is not known whether or not Francis noticed the prisoner on that particular day. In any event, the young man could not have guessed that the humble prisoner would one day be his religious leader.

The charge eventually brought against Ignatius concerned two women who had received spiritual guidance from him. A widow and her daughter, María del Vado and

Louisa Velásquez, had foolishly mixed piety with indiscre-tion. In their enthusiasm to devote their lives to charity, they had planned to travel from one hospital to another, until Ignatius forbade them to do so. However, they did not tell him of another planned venture: a pilgrimage with only a maidservant to the shrine of Our Lady of Guadalupe and of Saint Veronica at Jaen in Andalusia.

Setting off secretly one night in pilgrims' clothes, they aimed to reach Jaen for the traditional custom when the Santo Rostro, the sacred handkerchief of Saint Veronica, was displayed in the cathedral on Good Friday.

Their guardian, Don Pedro Guerillos, a professor of theology at the university, was incensed when he learned of his wards' irresponsible action. Knowing that they usu-ally confided in Ignatius, the professor assumed that Igna-tius was the architect of this escapade, and he immediately complained to Figueroa.

Ignatius' critics, quick to grab at anything that could denigrate him, enlarged on the affair. Tales were also con-cocted describing how women, under Ignatius' influence, were the victims of fainting fits, melancholia, and curious moods. There could be but one explanation; Ignatius must be the servant of the devil.

When Ignatius stood before Figueroa, he was asked if he and his disciples kept the Sabbath. Figueroa was clearly probing Ignatius' habit of devoting Saturdays (the Jewish Sabbath) toward honoring Our Lady. It was said that at that time in Spain some Jews professed to be Catholics but secretly tried to corrupt the Church from within.

Ignatius replied: "I keep the Sabbath in honor of the Blessed Virgin, but I know nothing of Jewish customs. . . ." He further denied any previous knowledge of the two women's intentions. But Figueroa wrongly insisted that Ignatius had introduced novelty into his talks to followers, whereupon Ignatius answered calmly: "My lord, I should have thought that it was no novelty to speak of Christ to Christians."

To all questions Ignatius supplied an appropriate answer, and when María del Vado and her daughter returned from Jaen, his innocence was firmly established. Yet, on July 1, after Ignatius' forty-two days' imprisonment, Figueroa issued two orders: Ignatius and his followers were to abandon their habits and wear normal students' dress; and at the risk of punishment, perhaps excommunication, they were to end public preaching or private conferences until they had completed their theological courses.

Replying to the first instruction, Ignatius said: "When you bade us dye our clothes, we did as we were told; but what you now order we cannot do because we have not money wherewith." Figueroa, however, was adamant, and he arranged for a priest to help Ignatius and his companions beg for money.

The question of clothing led to a curious incident. One of the people approached by a friend of Ignatius' was a merchant, Don Lopez de Mendoza. The merchant claimed that Ignatius was a rascal, adding: "May I be consumed by fire if he does not deserve to be burnt at the stake." That evening, while putting fireworks together to celebrate the birth of the infant prince of Spain, Mendoza accidentally ignited powder and died in the explosion.

To Ignatius, Figueroa's second instruction was frustrating and unjust. He had proved that he was blameless, yet

51

orders had been imposed. Moreover, even though it was temporary, the ban put an end for the time being to what would be his life's work: the salvation of souls.

Therefore, Ignatius tried to get the verdict reversed by consulting the archbishop of Toledo, Don Alonso Fonseca, then at Valladolid. The archbishop willingly agreed to repeal the sentence provided Ignatius made a formal appeal. But Ignatius declined. Instead, he said he would quit Alcalá and transfer to the University of Salamanca. The archbishop strongly advised this. Salamanca had been his own university. He had friends there, and he promptly offered to give letters of introduction. He also presented Ignatius with some money.

Thus, in the late summer of 1527, Ignatius left Alcalá with mixed feelings, for he was leaving both friends and enemies. His progress at the university had been poor, largely because he had tried to learn theology, physics, and logic at the same time. But there were other factors. There had been no proper system in his method of study. Too often it had been interrupted by his begging, his acts of charity for the sick and the poor, and his religious teaching. In addition, he had suffered persecutions.

As at Alcalá, Salamanca, the oldest university in Spain, catered to impoverished undergraduates. For that purpose, Bishop Diego de Anaya Maldonado had, in 1401, founded the College of San Bartolome, later called the Old College. "Lack of shirts and no superabundance of shoes" was the way Miguel de Cervantes described the Salamanca students. "Their dinner a penny piece of beef amongst four of them; a pottage made of the broth of the same, with salt and oatmeal and nothing else." Because there were no fires, before retiring to bed the students "were fain to walk or run up and down half an hour to get a heat into their feet."

As it turned out, Ignatius was unwise not to have appealed against the Inquisition's sentence. Salamanca belonged to the province of Valladolid, and, therefore, did not come within the authority of Toledo. And, like his disciples, Figueroa's verdict had gone on ahead before Ignatius arrived in the city. Thus, his activities were known to the authorities by the time he entered the university in July or August of 1527.

Only two weeks had elapsed when his Dominican confessor at the monastery of St. Stephen invited him to dinner the following Sunday. It seemed that the subprior wished to question him. After the meal, Ignatius, who was accompanied by Calixto, retired to the chapel with the subprior and two other monks. At the outset the subprior seemed to be affable, but he was curious to know why Calixto, whose garb did not fit well, was so oddly dressed. Ignatius explained that, acting on Figueroa's command, they had dispensed with their humble gowns and had begged for clothing.

When Ignatius admitted that he was uneducated and had scant knowledge of theology, the subprior grew hostile. Under the circumstances, insisted the subprior, in what way was Ignatius qualified to preach? Ignatius answered that he did not preach; he and his companions merely conversed with people about divine matters, encouraging them to shun vice and to practice virtue.

These were things, argued the subprior, of which no one

could speak unless he had been taught by the schools or by the Holy Spirit. Was it true that the Holy Ghost had revealed to Ignatius the subject of his discourses?

Ignatius was silent for some moments. The subprior, he felt, was too inquisitive. The recognized authorities of the Church were the ones entitled to probe whatever he did. The subprior had no such authority. Finally, Ignatius said: "Father, I will say no more than what I have said already, except before my superiors who have a right to interrogate me."

The reply so angered the subprior that Ignatius and Calixto were locked in the monastery. Yet they took their meals in the refectory and the brethren were permitted to visit them in their cell. The monks were sharply divided: some sympathized with the prisoners, realizing that the subprior—who had referred the matter to the Grand Vicar Frias—had exceeded his powers; the others supported the examination.

After three days Ignatius and Calixto were taken to the prison of the Inquisition. They were lodged in a fetid room above the common dungeon. Their feet were chained to a pillar, and, as Father Giovanni Polanco, Ignatius' future secretary, would one day record, "so they remained for the whole of the night in the company of small, most disgusting animals, which would not let them sleep."

The other followers, Caceres and Arteaga, were also arrested, but were committed to the dungeon. Only Jean was excused because of his youth. Frias interrogated each of the four men, Ignatius being last. He also examined the *Spiritual Exercises*.

After some days Ignatius faced a tribunal composed of

54

Frias and three doctors of theology. The judges asked him many questions on theological matters, such as the Eucharist, the Trinity, and Canon Law. Ignatius answered with such a breadth of knowledge that he amazed his examiners. No fault could be found with his replies. But what they dwelt upon was a definition in the *Spiritual Exercises* relating to pardonable and mortal sin. How, they asked, could anyone be so bold as to preach on such intricate matters without having previously been instructed in theology?

Ignatius listened patiently, then declared that the issue was not whether he was qualified to comment but whether he spoke the truth. "Whether what I have said is true or not, that is for you to judge. If then it be not true, condemn the definition."

The Inquisitors significantly ignored the challenge. Instead, they asked Ignatius to illustrate his method of teaching by talking on the First Commandment. As they listened to the humble man speaking so beautifully on God's love, they marveled and respected him.

This did not mean that Ignatius was at once released. He and his companions remained locked up for another twenty-two days. But they were allowed to receive visitors. One nobleman—later cardinal bishop of Burgos—asked how Ignatius could tolerate unjustified suffering in chains. Ignatius answered that the question exposed him as having little love of Christ if he could not endure bonds for Christ's sake. "Salamanca," he said, "has no fetters, manacles, and chains so many as I long to wear for God."

The Inquisitors discharged the prisoners, but forbade them to instruct on complex questions or to distinguish between mortal and venial sin. Ignatius emphatically refused to comply. To obey would prevent him from speaking to people about good and evil.

Polanco wrote: "One of the judges who was most favorably disposed toward him jumped to his feet and asked him what he found in the verdict to displease him. Ignatius replied that, seeing they did not declare what he taught about mortal and venial sin to be false, they had no grounds for imposing on him silence on this point. And he added that he would rather leave Salamanca than conform to that verdict."

CHAPTER 7

IN PARIS

After his experiences in Alcalá and Salamanca, Ignatius at last knew that the Inquisition would ban his teaching, although no fault could be found with it. No matter where he went in Spain this attitude would prevail. There was no alternative; although his stay at Salamanca had been a mere two months, he must leave the country. Where could he go?

He discussed the problem with his companions. Perhaps, he thought, there would be greater freedom in France. Furthermore, he could pursue his studies at the university in Paris. His followers would stay at Salamanca until he sent for them.

Thus, three weeks after leaving prison, Ignatius gathered his books and manuscripts, and began the journey to Barcelona. There his friends tried to dissuade him from continuing on to Paris. France and Spain were at war and, they warned, the route over the Pyrenees would be filled with danger. Robbers were taking advantage of the chaos. Atrocities were not uncommon, and it was rumored that the

French were even committing Spaniards to the oven. Ignatius, however, was heedless of his friends' anxieties.

Alone, he began the wearisome journey of some five hundred miles. It was midwinter and the days were short. He traveled along the lonely tracks and passes of the Pyrenees, now thick with snow, and on February 2, 1528—a cold and damp day—he arrived safely in the French capital.

So that he could devote more time to his studies, Ignatius had accepted money from his benefactors in Barcelona. At least he would not lose valuable time by having to beg. Taking accommodations near the university, he joined the many thousands of students who attended the sixty colleges and schools south of the Seine.

The students were divided into four groups: French, Picard, Norman, and German, each with its own procurator. The French came from southern France, Italy, and Spain; the Picards from Flanders and Brabant; the Normans from northern France; and the Germans (until the Hundred Years' War this division had been called English) from northern European countries.

Studying grammar, Ignatius first attended the College of Montaigu where Erasmus, years earlier, had complained because of bad eggs. And at the time of Ignatius' enrollment John Calvin had not much longer to remain at the college. This was a strange coincidence, for both Erasmus and Calvin would help to inspire the new religion against which Ignatius' future followers would one day struggle. It was during the year after Ignatius reached Paris that Calvin was suddenly converted.

The College of Montaigu had a reputation for discipline, a fact that perhaps appealed to Ignatius. Someone described the college as enjoying "a reputation of great austerity and discipline; behavior there is as good as in church; for that reason whenever a boy who lives in Paris is wayward and hard to manage, he is packed off to Montaigu and brought under the rod of humility and obedience."

Apparently the other colleges were not so orderly. For instance, a quite different scene was depicted by George Buchanan, the Scottish scholar who taught grammar and Latin literature for some years at the nearby College of Sainte Barbe. He recorded:

While the professor is puffing over his teaching, these crazy boys go to sleep or into daydreams of play and amusement. One boy stays away and has bribed his neighbor to answer for him; another has lost his stocking; a third is gazing at his foot that peeps out from a hole in his boot; a fourth pretends to be ill; a fifth is writing home. No help but in the rod; then sobbing and tear-stained cheeks for the rest of the day. Now a troop of loafers from the district across the river tramps in; the clatter of hobnail boots announces their approach. . . . They are ill-humored because they did not notice the announcement of the course, although it is placarded at the street corners, and they are offended because the professor does not read out of an enormous tome scribbled all over with marginal comments. So they all get up and with an infernal hubbub walk across the way to Montaigu, where the odor of soap pervades.

The charity of his Spanish friends allowed Ignatius to

live at an inn close to the Seine. But he had grown unaccustomed to having money, and he did not care to carry it with him. Living at the inn was a fellow Spanish student, Ferdinand Mazores, with whom Ignatius was friendly. Mazores was poor, but—so Ignatius believed—trustworthy. He asked Mazores to take care of his gold coins, and the Spaniard agreed to do so.

But Ignatius was unwise in his choice of a custodian. When the time came to pay the rent, Mazores was unable to produce the money. Not only had he spent it, but he could not replace it.

Ignatius had considered spending some of the coins to bring his disciples from Spain. Yet this was now out of the question. So he wrote to them telling them to complete their studies at Salamanca. As time would show, the association between Ignatius and his first followers would deteriorate; each of the disciples would cease to imitate his leader and would go his own way. Calixto eventually entered the merchant service and voyaged twice to the West Indies. Caceres went back to his native Segovia, and his subsequent fate is not known. Arteaga attained high office in the Church. As a bishop in the Indies, he died on October 8, 1540, in Mexico, from accidental poisoning. Juanico joined a religious order.

Now deprived of his money, Ignatius was confronted with the lot of other poor students: to seek a place that offered free lodgings, and to beg for food. This was no new experience, and being a slave to poverty, it actually brought him happiness. He managed to get a room in a poorhouse, but it was an appreciable distance from the college. This arrangement inevitably interfered with his studies. To begin with, there was a strict enforcement of rules, such as a regulation that prevented him from leaving the house before sunrise or after nightfall. This interfered with his studies because lectures in winter started before sunrise and afternoon lectures continued until darkness. So he necessarily had to sacrifice part of them.

It was not surprising, therefore, that Ignatius again made no substantial progress. This gave him much concern. To make headway he had tried to place himself at the service of a professor; when he was not engaged in domestic duties he had hoped to allocate his time toward studying. His search, however, yielded no such transaction.

Finally, he abandoned this idea in favor of a journey during the summer vacation to Flanders—that part of Spanish territory closest to Paris. Bruges and Antwerp were busy commercial centers, and attracted wealthy Spanish merchants. They responded so well to Ignatius' pleas that he collected sufficient alms to maintain himself, in a humble way, for a year.

He was now able to quit the poorhouse and live in the College of Sainte Barbe where, in October, 1529, he started a course in philosophy. Now he no longer had to beg from door to door, and he applied himself more assiduously to study. In a similar way he raised money during the next two years. In the third year he crossed the English Channel and in London met with a much more generous response. After that the merchants in Flanders, admiring Ignatius' virtue, sent alms to him in Paris.

Meanwhile, Ignatius had other problems to contend with. Once he had established himself at the university he renewed his practice of giving the Spiritual Exercises.

61

Three well-to-do students and fellow countrymen joined him: Juan de Castro, Pedro de Peralta, and Amadores, a Biscayan. They all lived at Sainte Barbe and insisted on molding their lives after Ignatius'. They sold all their possessions—including their books—and distributed the money among the poor. Then they took a vow of poverty. They did so of their own volition, for the Exercises forbade any attempt to influence others.

The result of the students' actions was to get Ignatius into trouble. He had gone to Rouen, having learned that Mazores was sick and destitute. Ignatius walked the distance in three days, and then begged for his friend. Next he arranged for him to return by ship to Spain, and wrote to Calixto and Arteaga requesting them to help him.

Ignatius was still in Rouen when he received a letter from Paris; a complaint, it warned, had been lodged against him with the Inquisition. Dr. Pedro Ortiz, the tutor of Castro and Peralta, and Dr. Diego de Govea, the rector of Sainte Barbe, wished to have his activities investigated. His evangelism was under suspicion. Moreover, the news that he had been interrogated by the Spanish Inquisition had spread to France.

So that no one could suspect him of having gone to Rouen to escape, Ignatius secured a certificate from a notary testifying that he had left for Paris immediately after receiving the complaint. Back in Paris he at once approached the inquisitor, Dr. Matteo Ori, a Dominican friar, requesting him to examine the charges without delay; he was due to begin his philosophy course, but he wished to do so without anxiety.

Ori's examination proved Ignatius' innocence. But he

suffered the loss of the three new followers. Yielding to pressure from relations and friends, they abandoned their vows of poverty. In due time, Castro joined the Carthusian Order, and Peralta entered the priesthood to become a canon of Toledo. It is not known what happened to Amadores.

At Sainte Barbe, Ignatius shared a room with two other students: Peter Favre from Savoy and Francis Xavier, a Spaniard from Navarre. Xavier planned to teach philosophy, but his association with Ignatius was to change his career.

In the meantime, Ignatius was trying to concentrate more on his studies than on converts. Even so, many students began to emulate him, with the result that it upset the college life. It was customary on feast days for students to participate in public disputation as part of their education. But now many preferred to pray and take the sacraments instead. These disruptions caused Ignatius' tutor, Father Juan Pena, to admonish him. But Ignatius denied that he deliberately tried to create disorder. "I merely mind my own business," he said, "but other people want to imitate me."

This, however, was not all. Foolishly, even though humanly, Ignatius had nursed someone who was sick with the plague. While dressing the man's sores, a sharp pain had run through one of Ignatius' hands. He had feared that he, too, was stricken, and to make up for his immediate horror he had clapped his hand into his mouth, crying: "If you have the plague in your hand, you shall have it in your mouth also."

Ignatius had not been affected. Yet, when it was known

at the college what he had done it struck terror into both professors and students.

Finally, Pena lost his patience and reported Ignatius to Dr. Govea, who, to discipline him, decided on a public birching. Ignatius was so accustomed to inflicting physical pain upon himself that the prospect of a beating did not worry him. It was the flogging in public that he angrily resented; it would bring ridicule to his religious ideals.

Thus, while the students were assembling to witness the whipping, Ignatius went to see the rector in his room. "As regards myself," he told Govea, "I could desire nothing more than to bear stripes and shame for the sake of Jesus Christ, as indeed I have borne imprisonment and chains, and have never uttered a word in my defense, nor would I permit anyone to plead for me.

"But now it is not my interest or honor only that is at stake, but the eternal salvation of numerous souls. I ask you whether it be an act of Christian justice to permit a man to be publicly disgraced whose only crime is to have labored to make the name of Jesus better known and loved? Is it right, as you would answer before God, to put this open shame upon me solely with a view to detaching from me those whom I have drawn to myself only that I might bring them to God?"

Govea was a stern but just person. He now realized that, in these circumstances, punishment would do more harm than good. Tradition claims that, affected by Ignatius' words, Govea went with him to the hall, and before the astonished students he meekly sought pardon for his hastiness.

Although it is generally accepted that Govea's apology

is legend and not fact, Ignatius was not whipped. Years later Govea ardently supported the Jesuits and influenced King John III of Portugal to enlist the services of this order for missionary activity in Goa.

Ignatius' supporters now included Pena and other professors. In his enthusiasm, the professor of philosophy wanted Ignatius to begin studying theology at once, but Ignatius preferred to finish the philosophy course first. He was not making any effort to convert people, yet his persuasive gifts and force of personality were unwittingly reacting on others.

Various stories linger to illustrate this. One concerned a doctor of theology who invited Ignatius to play billiards with him. Ignatius said he would agree, provided that there was a stake. Being poor, he pointed out that he owned nothing beyond his own person. "If then I lose," he said, "I will be your servant for a month to obey your orders. If I win you shall do just one thing for me, and it shall be something to your advantage."

The doctor willingly consented, but lost the game. Now revealing his terms, Ignatius asked his opponent to read the *Spiritual Exercises* for one month. The outcome was a marked change in the doctor's life.

There is also the tale about the priest who led a shameful life. Falling on his knees before him, Ignatius was so penitent when confessing his sins that the priest, who had hitherto been indifferent to his own worse sins, was overcome by a sense of disgrace. Pleading for Ignatius' help to lead a more worthy existence, he was introduced to the *Spiritual Exercises*.

CHAPTER 8

THE VOW AT MONTMARTRE

In the main, Ignatius' influence on others in Paris had been quite unintentional. As yet his Company of Jesus consisted solely of himself. Probably he wondered if he would ever found his movement, for wherever he went he encountered the frustrations of failure and obstruction. His previous companions had abandoned him. Lacking his leadership, the first three had grown disinterested. The next three had wilted before the violent anger of others who had vehemently argued that the youths had disgraced their families.

However, Ignatius need not have worried. The future nucleus of his Society already existed in his college room. Because Ignatius encountered so many vexing difficulties in the philosophy course, Pena asked Peter Favre to be a tutor.

Born of humble parents at Villaret, a little mountain village not far from Geneva, Favre was already an advanced student when Ignatius began the course. From the age of twelve Favre had dedicated himself to a religious career. Even in childhood he would ardently preach to the peasants in his locality. But the priesthood seemed very remote. Favre tended the family sheep until, avid for learning, his father was induced to have him educated. A Carthusian relative had eased the way to Paris.

Favre was now twenty-four, and Ignatius was fifteen years his senior. Whereas the younger man had a superior intellectual capacity, the older man was much better endowed in a spiritual sense. Favre was conscious of this when he and Ignatius discussed Pena's lectures.

At that time Favre, like Ignatius at Manresa, was troubled by a disturbing mental conflict. He found it difficult to resist the worldly pleasures of Paris, and he was in danger of breaking a vow he had taken in childhood. And so he asked Ignatius to guide him through the Spiritual Exercises. He made them with zeal but indulged in excessive mortification. For instance, he fasted for days at a time, and during an extremely bitter winter he inflicted punishment on himself by kneeling in a freezing courtyard throughout the night.

Favre was wholly converted, and at his own request became Ignatius' first permanent disciple. On accepting him, Ignatius ordered him to eat regularly and not torture himself with the cold.

Had anyone told Francis Xavier that he, too, would be enrolled, he would have scoffed at the idea. A brilliant scholar, Xavier was ambitious to achieve triumphs in the teaching world. Having graduated, he was lecturing on Aristotle at the College of Beauvais in Paris, where he was already establishing a high reputation. A dazzling scholastic future lay ahead, yet he would become one of the greatest missionaries of all time.

Ignatius' roommates were of a contrasting social background. Whereas Favre came of peasant stock, Xavier was

68

born, on April 7, 1506, in the castle of Xavier near San-guesa in Navarre. He was the youngest son of Juan de Jassu, who had been president of the royal council of the last French kings of Navarre. But loyalty to the Court through varying fortunes had impoverished his family. Francis' two older brothers, Miguel and Juan, had entered the army, and by coincidence had served in the force that stormed Pamplona when Ignatius was wounded.

As a companion, Xavier was aloof, even contemptuous, of Ignatius' mediocre academic skill. Also, unlike Xavier, Ignatius was not an athlete. From Xavier's attitude, it was obvious to Ignatius that the young nobleman thought of him as a humble crank. Yet Ignatius persisted with his gentle friendliness.

What Ignatius lacked in a scholastic sense he gained in his knowledge and treatment of men. He wisely appealed to the young professor's weakness: his pride. Moreover, he eulogized Xavier's talents to others and even recruited pupils for him. Gradually, the barrier of aloofness broke down, but the conversion was slow.

The time when Xavier—until then the erudite young pro-fessor—began to think profoundly of spiritual things dates from a conversation in which Ignatius quoted Christ's words: "What shall it profit a man if he gain the whole world and suffer the loss of his own soul?" Xavier reflected on this saying and it changed the course of his life. He asked to be the second disciple. In so doing, Ignatius made the greatest recruiting conversion of his life. He himself had visualized years of evangelizing among the heathen, but that would be the task fulfilled by Xavier.

Wishing to see his son establish a career in Spain,

Xavier's father sent for him, but the young man declined to return. His sister Magdalena, a nun in the Convent of St. Clare at Gandia, supported him, prophesying: "God has chosen him to be his messenger to the Indies, and a strong pillar of his Church."

Francis' decision to follow Ignatius was unpopular with certain of his friends, who attached the blame to Ignatius. One of them, Miguel Navarro, even proposed to murder him. Scaling a ladder, dagger in hand, Navarro had reached Ignatius' window when what appeared to be a voice—perhaps merely his conscience—questioned his actions. Navarro was so terrified that, leaping into the room, he threw himself at Ignatius' feet and pleaded for forgiveness.

Quite unexpectedly, Ignatius received two more recruits. Diego Laínez of Almazan in Castile and Alfonso Salmerón of Toledo, both studying at the University of Alcalá, had heard conflicting reports about Ignatius. Some extolled him for his saintliness, others accused him of being a sectary—someone who has ulterior motives which might harm the Church. Deciding to find out for themselves, they went to Paris, and by a strange coincidence, the first person they met was Ignatius. He found lodgings for them and very soon the youths, who would one day be papal theologians, volunteered to join him.

The little group now comprised five members. Soon there would be a sixth. Because Nicholás Alfonso had no surname, he had come to be known as Bobadilla, after the village near Leonese Palencia in Spain, where he was born. He had lectured on philosophy at Valladolid and now proposed to study theology in Paris. He, too, fell under Ignatius' spell.

70

Next came another scholar, Simón Rodriguez, a Portuguese nobleman from Voucella. When he was a child, his dying father had predicted future distinction for him in the Church. Rodriguez had been attracted to Ignatius because of his plan to evangelize in the Holy Land.

But during this period Ignatius failed to recruit the only man he ever deliberately set out to enlist in his Society. This was Jerome Nadal, a Majorcan, who was a hospital patient when Ignatius met him. Ignatius admired Nadal's qualities so much that, breaking his rule, he besought him to join his movement.

In his autobiography, Nadal recalls: "He took me to the little old church that is near the gate of St. Jacques, and by the baptismal font read me a long letter that he had written to some nephew of his in Spain, of which the purport was to win him from the world to a life of perfection. The Devil perceived very well the efficacy of the letter and of its writer, and dragged me forcibly from the spiritual power that sought me. So, as we went out and were standing within the space in front of the church door, I said to Ignatius (I had the New Testament in my hands), 'I propose to follow this book; I don't know in what direction you are headed; please do not do any more in this matter and don't concern yourself about me.'"

The incident taught Ignatius the folly of trying to persuade anyone to a vocation. Years later he would be noted for the way he at times turned away novices. Sometimes he summarily expelled them, even dragging them out of their beds at night.

Ten years were to elapse before Nadal realized his vocation, sometime around 1540. On seeing a copy of a letter from Francis Xavier, who was then a missionary in India, Nadal was so impressed that he journeyed to Rome, made the Spiritual Exercises, and became a Jesuit.

Although few in number, the Jesuits started to function as a body after Ignatius passed his final examination at Easter in 1534, at the age of forty-three. He was now a Master of Arts, the outcome of a decade of dogged study.

So far Ignatius and his six companions—Favre, Xavier, Laínez, Salmerón, Bobadilla, and Rodriguez—had talked vaguely of what they would do in the days ahead, but now it was necessary to make precise plans. What should be the pattern of their future? Speaking to each of his companions privately, Ignatius asked them to decide on a given day, after a period of fasting and prayer.

It was at dawn on August 15, 1534, the Feast of the Assumption, that the companions left the city and went up the hill of Montmartre, which is today surmounted by the massive basilica of the Sacré Coeur. Roughly halfway up the hill they entered the small deserted chapel of Our Lady of Montmartre, the site of the martyrdom of Saint Denis.

In that quiet setting, Ignatius first said a prayer and then outlined his intentions. He was determined, he said, to go to the Holy Land, there to serve God under vows of poverty and chastity.

The others readily expressed their willingness to accompany him. All agreed that should objections arise to their residing in Palestine, they should vote on whether they should stay and bear the hardships or return to Rome where they would tender their services to the pope. Meanwhile, there would be no pilgrimage until all had completed their studies.

This meant that the venture was to be delayed for three years. All seven were to meet in Venice on January 25, 1537, and embark for Jerusalem. If by chance a voyage should prove impossible they reiterated their intention to go to Rome and put themselves at His Holiness's disposal. To renew their vows, they were to meet again in Montmartre on the same feast day for the next two years.

Out of that simple discussion, in a chapel on Montmartre hill, the Jesuit movement was truly born. In the cool light of daybreak the little party descended to the crypt beneath the church, where Favre, the only priest among them, said Mass. As they knelt before the altar and received Holy Communion, they each in turn repeated aloud their vows of poverty, chastity, and total obedience to the pope. Each would journey to the Holy Land. When each was ordained a priest, no payment would be accepted for any form of pious service.

On leaving the chapel they went to a fountain at the foot of the hill. Now bound together by a common purpose, they spent the day there, contemplating their future service to God.

CHAPTER 9

RENDEZVOUS IN VENICE

Unlike the others, Ignatius never completed his theological studies in Paris. Illness once again overtook him. The lack of proper nourishment had badly affected his digestion. Like an echo of his days at Manresa, he had returned once more to acute asceticism, spending many hours praying and meditating in the Carmelite church of Montmartre and in the nearby gypsum quarries.

Advised by his doctors, he prepared to leave for Spain, hoping that the air would restore his health. There was also another reason for his departure. Xavier, Laínez, and Salmerón had family matters to attend to in order to comply with their vows of poverty. Thus, they gave Ignatius power of attorney to complete their affairs.

But before he left, gossip again led to his appearance before the Inquisition. This time he was accused of trying to found a new heretical sect. The evidence, however, was so baseless that Laurent, the inquisitor, soon realized the futility of the charge. To the chagrin of his accusers, he willingly gave Ignatius an official certificate declaring that

75

he was not guilty of heresy. On January 23, 1535, Laurent wrote:

> We, Brother Thomas Laurent, professor of theology, priest of the Order of Preaching Brothers, Inquisitor-General in France, delegated by the Holy See, certify by these presents that after an inquiry made by our precursor, Valentine Leivon, and by his council, into the life, morals and doctrine of Ignatius of Loyola, we have found nothing that is not Catholic and Christian; we also know the said Loyola, and M. Peter Favre and some of his friends, and we have always seen them live in a Catholic and virtuous manner, and observed nothing in them but what becomes a Christian and virtuous man. The *Exercises* also which the said Loyola teaches seem to us, so far as we have looked into them, to be Catholic.

Riding a mount supplied by his companions, Ignatius began the journey to Spain about the end of March, 1535. After he was recognized at Bayonne, news of his coming went ahead to his family at Loyola. Joyfully, Don Martin sent an escort to greet him, but, being pledged to poverty, Ignatius evaded his ancestral home. Instead, he went straight to Azpeitia, lodging at the Hospital of St. Maddelena. He even declined the comfortable bed and the provisions brought by Don Martin's servants. Ignatius spent only one night at the castle of Loyola, responding to the plea of Doña Magdalena, his sister-in-law.

So that parents and relations should not encroach upon the disciples' love of Christ, Ignatius compelled his followers to forsake their families. In his own case he had stuck paper over a picture of the Blessed Virgin in his prayer book, because it reminded him of Doña Magdalena. When Ignatius revealed that he proposed to preach to the people, Don Martin told him it would be pointless; no one, he said, would come to listen. Yet Ignatius' words drew so many that he was compelled to leave the town and speak to the crowd in the countryside. In his simple, forceful language, he condemned the dissolute ways of the priests, and ousted the vice of gambling, which was rife in the community. For the next three years neither dice nor cards were seen in the town.

Ignatius also attacked the wearing of unseemly female dress and revived the ancient custom of ringing the church bell for prayer three times daily. As a result of his visit, private relief would be organized for poor people who were too shy to beg or proclaim their poverty.

One resolve that had brought him back to Azpeitia was to compensate the unfortunate man who had suffered imprisonment after Ignatius and others had robbed an orchard many years earlier. Publicly expressing his guilt, Ignatius, as if to settle a long-standing debt, signed papers transferring his two farms to the man.

Ignatius had remained for three months in Azpeitia when, his health restored, he left his native town. He would never see it again. Don Martin accompanied him to the Biscayan border, then Ignatius carried on alone. He had much to do. For there were business affairs to settle for his three disciples at Xavier, Almazan, and Toledo. He wished, too, to visit Juan de Castro, now a Carthusian novice at Segovia.

During his travels Ignatius met a nine-year-old boy who would one day be crowned Philip II of Spain. With prophetic insight, the child's nurse told the future king to ask for Ignatius' prayers. "That," she observed, "is a saint." It indicated that Ignatius by now had achieved some measure of fame in his own country.

His duties fulfilled, he went to the port of Valencia and, surviving a storm, eventually arrived in Genoa. The journey on foot during winter over the Apennines to Bologna was also eventful. One day he suddenly found himself on the edge of a precipice. He could go neither backward nor forward, but was forced perilously to clamber up a steep rock on his hands and knees. One slip and he would have crashed to his death.

On entering Bologna, he was less fortunate. He fell from a bridge into the water. Soaked and in poor health, and also the butt of noisy urchins' jokes, he was given care and comfort in the Spanish College.

Ignatius reached Venice on the last day of 1535. While waiting for his companions from Paris he continued his theological studies and evangelism. This city of canals yielded one more follower, a Spaniard, Diego Hozes, who was also a priest from Andalusia.

Before they left Paris on November 15, 1536, his disciples added three more recruits to their numbers: Paschase Broët from Bretancourt, Claude Le Jay of Savoy, and Jean Codure, a layman from Provence.

Shabbily dressed, with their skirts stuffed into their belts, this rather odd-looking party passed from France into Lorraine. On leaving Metz they traveled to Basle and Constance. In France they endured frequent rain, and in Germany and Switzerland the roads thick with snow added to their hardships. The journey over the Alps was extremely taxing.

To undertake so laborious a journey on foot in winter was arduous enough, but renewed war between France and Spain created other anxieties. There was also the threat from Protestantism, the new religion that was winning adherents in parts of Europe. One such region contained the Swiss provinces through which they passed. Once encountering a company of French soldiers, the party was saved from possible harm by a peasant who cried: "Can't you see these men are reformers? Can't you see that they are going to reform some country?"

Somehow in the Protestant villages they managed to find someone who came to their aid. Once when it seemed that they would be imprisoned near Constance, a young German visited the inn in which they were lodged and guided them safely across the snow to the road to Constance.

It was on January 6, 1537, that Ignatius, who had been in Venice for about a year, was reunited with all his disciples. No ships would sail for the Holy Land until the spring. Therefore, they split up into two groups, one engaging in works of charity at the Hospital of Saints John and Paul and the other at the Hospital of Nicholas.

Believing that it would be advisable to outline their plan to the pope before leaving for the Levant, all—save Ignatius and Hozes—started for Rome in mid-Lent. Ignatius stayed behind because there were now two men at the papal court who, he believed, were not favorably disposed toward him. These two were Ortiz, who had denounced him to the Inquisition in Paris, and Cardinal Juan Caraffa, patron of the Theatine Order, which Ignatius and Hozes had refused to join. If they saw him or Hozes in Rome, Ignatius feared that they would be hostile to his venture.

The journey to Rome was full of hardships. Traveling three by three, with a priest in each group, the nine men had to contend with considerable rain and floodwaters. They were even forced to wade up to their waists. As usual they owned no money and begged for their food. Sometimes this was no more than bread and water. And once, while passing a pinewood at Ravenna, they relied on a diet of pinecones.

It was remarkable how these men, especially those who had known affluence, could tolerate such conditions. At Ancona, one of the travelers was obliged to pawn his breviary. Subsequently, he wrote: "When I was passing through the streets of Ancona, begging alms with which I might redeem my breviary, I saw one of my companions, wet and barefooted, asking the market woman to give him in charity a little fruit and vegetables. I thought of his high birth, his great talents, the riches he had renounced, the eminent learning and virtue which would have given him such influence in the world; and I felt unworthy to be the associate of such men."

Father Simón Rodriguez recorded another instance of the type of forbidding situations that Jesuits persistently experienced. It occurred in Ravenna. He wrote:

It happened that three of the companions went to the same hospital. The beds offered them had been much used and were very dirty, the sheets were foul and badly spotted with blood. Nevertheless, two of them, one with his clothes on, the other stripped, were not afraid to get in. The third [believed to be Rodriguez], kept back by horror of the filth, sought another spot. But . . . he reflected on what he had done, and grieved greatly that he had shirked in the battle. He laid it to weakness, self-indulgence, and delicacy of body, and mightily desired that a new occasion would offer itself in which he might retrieve the flabby act. God did not fail him. For when he and another brother arrived at the hospital of some village, the matron informed them that there was no bed except one which a patient had occupied who had died that day of the lousy disease. The sheets, she said, were clean, for the patient had not used them while alive, but they had been laid under his dead body, out of respect for the cross and for the priests who had come to the infirmary to say the last rites and bury the body.

The matron did not exaggerate; the sheets had been spilled with holy water, and were thick with great big lice which accompany that disease. The Father, who had once been vanquished, now saw his way to win a victory over himself, and seized the opportunity. He took off all his clothes and jumped quickly between the sheets. The lice rushed incontinently upon him, pinched and stung him all night long, and made his body smart till it sweated. Of a truth the Father conquered himself, he conquered and won the field gloriously. His companion also laid down in the same place but kept his clothes on.

In Rome the party was surprised to discover that Ortiz,

rather than being hostile, insisted on personally introducing them to Pope Paul III. His Holiness asked Favre and his colleagues to hold a theological disputation during dinner one evening and was greatly impressed by their wealth of knowledge and humility.

The pope readily gave them leave to visit the Holy Land. "But I do not think you will go," he said. The Holy Father had in mind the strife between the Venetians and the Turks. The pope also granted another request; the companions who so far were not priests could receive Holy Orders from any bishop. Salmerón, who was still too young, was accorded the special privilege of becoming a priest at the age of twenty-three. Paul also presented them with fifty crowns to help them on their journey to Jerusalem.

When Ignatius heard the good news he suggested that they should renew their vows before Monsignor Verallo, the papal legate. Then, responding to the pope's magnanimity, they received the priesthood from the bishop of Arba on June 24, 1537, the Feast of St. John the Baptist.

Owing to the war with the Turks, the companions now agreed to wait a year before attempting the voyage to the Levant. In the meantime, they would disperse for forty days to make retreats. Ignatius was accompanied by Favre and Laínez to Vicenza, and the rest scattered to Monselice, Monte Celso, Bassano, Verona, and Treviso. Near Vicenza, Ignatius and his companions found a deserted monastic house that gave them the required solitude for prayer and meditation. Later they preached in the streets, much to the amusement of the crowds, who laughed at their poor Italian. But they drew the people by shouting and waving their hats.

While Ignatius was at Vicenza, Rodriguez and Le Jay were admitted into the cell of a hermit named Antonio, in San Vito, near Bassano. Taken ill, Rodriguez was thought to have little longer to live. And so in company with Favre, Ignatius, himself sick with fever, went to visit him. On the way Ignatius turned to Favre and said: "Rodriguez will not die." He prophesied correctly.

After Rodriguez recovered, the company made their temporary home in Bassano. Rodriguez, however, felt unsettled, disliking the hurly-burly of the city. He longed to go back to the peace and solitude of Antonio's cell. It induced him to believe that his place was not with the companions, but that he should withdraw from the world for meditation. He secretly left Bassano to return to the hermit's cell, but on the way a man with a sword came toward him. The threatening figure seemed no normal being, and the terrified Rodriguez fled back to Bassano. Ignatius welcomed him with Christ's words: "O thou of little faith why dost thou doubt?"

CHAPTER 10

SERVANTS OF THE POPE

Their goal was still the Holy Land, but the war continued and it was too hazardous for ships to venture into Adriatic waters. Summer passed, the autumn days slipped by, and as winter approached, the prospect of the pilgrimage dimmed.

During September the companions gathered at Vicenza where all of the new priests with the exception of Ignatius and Rodriguez said their first Mass. Ignatius waited for more than a year—until Christmas of 1538—to say Mass in the Chapel of the Nativity in Santa Maria. Rodriguez said his first Mass the following year at Ferrara.

Ignatius and his followers had almost completed their year, and it was now necessary once more to consider the future. He interpreted the obstruction between themselves and the Holy Land as a sign that God did not wish them to go there. It was the first time in many years that pilgrims had not been able to journey to Jerusalem. What should they do now? They had agreed earlier that Rome would be the alternative to Jerusalem, and this was again confirmed. They would appear before the pope and, as his servants, fulfill whatever he bade them do.

Ignatius also considered that they should try to recruit students to their way of life. So it was arranged that Ignatius, Favre, and Laínez should journey to Rome, while the others visited university centers in northern Italy and gave the Exercises. Le Jay and Rodriguez would go to Ferrara; Broët and Salmerón to Siena; Xavier and Bobadilla to Bologna; and Codure and Hozes to Padua.

All were to depend on alms, and they were to live in hospitals. To insure equality in each pair, every week one was to be the superior of the other. As well as preaching, they would work among the sick.

For the first time an important query arose. What name were they to give if they were asked to describe themselves? Ignatius ordained that they should reply that they belonged to the Company (later Society) of Jesus.

Very soon the Company was to lose one of its members. In Padua, Hozes and Codure were imprisoned, being suspected by the local clergy of heresy. They were released, however, the following day. Not long afterward Hozes preached on the text: "Watch and pray, for ye know neither the day nor the hour." His words were extremely applicable to himself, for Hozes, ravaged by fever, died not long afterward in hospital. Le Jay took his place.

Before the Company had dispersed, Xavier had also been ill with fever. His sickness had been marked by a vision of Saint Jerome, who foretold that in Bologna Xavier would be given a cross that would benefit his soul. This, indeed, took place. After Xavier said Mass in the chapel that is the burial place of Saint Dominic, a lady spoke to him and induced him to live with her uncle, Giraloma Casalia, a canon of St. Petronius. There Xavier was ill for some months with fever, the cross predicted by Saint Jerome. On recovering he gained distinction for his apostolic work in Bologna.

An even more strange incident involved Ignatius on his way to Rome. At La Storta, six miles from the city, he experienced perhaps the most astonishing of his many visions. Praying in a hermitage chapel, he saw Jesus bearing his cross, and Our Lord said to him: "I will be propitious to you in Rome."

At first Ignatius did not know how to interpret these words. The cross perhaps implied that he would suffer a martyr's fate. He told Favre and Laínez: "I do not know what awaits us at Rome; I do not know whether it is the will of God that we should die by crucifixion or on the rack. I know only one thing—that Jesus will be propitious there."

They reached Rome toward the end of November, 1537. Laínez removed his shoes and entered barefoot. When they were shown into the pope's chambers, Paul III welcomed their services with enthusiasm. At a time when forces were undermining the Church, the pope saw in the Jesuits an instrument that would help counter them. The word "Jesuit" was first used by others as a nickname of ridicule. But when the Society was accepted it became the normal name for a member.

This was Ignatius' first meeting with the Supreme Pontiff, who listened with kindness as Ignatius asked him to use his Company in whatever way he wished. The pope wasted no time; Favre, he said, would teach the Scriptures at the College of Sapienza, and Laínez would lecture on scholastic theology there. Ignatius was to concentrate on preaching to the people and giving the Spiritual Exercises.

Very soon the three men were a subject of conversation in Roman life. Many listened admiringly to them, but the Marquis d'Aguilar, the imperial ambassador, warned that certain people charged them with heresy. A facade of humility, it was being alleged, merely concealed the Jesuits' ambitions for high office. The insinuation prompted Ignatius to declare that neither he nor any of his followers would ever accept ecclesiastical honors except to comply with the pope's instructions.

Despite these criticisms, the three Jesuits made a remarkable impact on Rome. Many people were keen to make the Spiritual Exercises, among them the powerful Cardinal Contrarini, the ambassador from Siena, who, like the pope, brought about reforms in the Church. The cardinal wholeheartedly supported Ignatius and on Contrarini's recommendation, Dr. Ortiz, who had been hostile to the Jesuits, traveled to Monte Cassino with Ignatius and there made the Exercises under his guidance.

It was while they were there that Hozes died in Padua. Ignatius later recorded that he was aware of the death, and claimed that he witnessed the spirit of his former disciple borne up to Heaven by angels.

The Company would still number eleven—Ignatius, Favre, Xavier, Laínez, Salmerón, Bobadilla, Rodriguez, Broët, Le Jay, Codure, and a new recruit, Francis Strada. Recently in the service of Cardinal Caraffa, Strada, who would gain fame by his eloquent preaching, had intended to leave for Naples as a soldier of fortune, but Ignatius had changed Strada's mind in Rome.

Now, at Ignatius' request, all the companions returned to Rome during Lent, 1538. They were accommodated in a house in the neighborhood of Santa Trinità dei Monti. But because their quarters were so cramped, they moved to bigger premises in the Piazza Margana near the center of Rome.

Each day they were seen preaching in the city's streets or churches and begging for alms. Schoolmasters even took their scholars to hear them preach. An Augustinian friar named Agostino was also attracting attention by his Lenten preaching. Secretly he was devoted to the teachings of Martin Luther, whose new religion was undermining the Catholic Church.

Salmerón and Laínez noticed that in his sermons Agostino subtly introduced heretical teaching. They argued with him in private without avail, but this was enough to make Agostino realize that the Jesuits presented a serious threat.

Agostino, therefore, defamed Ignatius by distorting his past. He described him as a wolf disguised as a shepherd, who had committed frightful ravages in several of the universities of Europe under the mask of sanctity. "But even in Rome," he declared, "there are men of incorruptible faith, belonging to his own nation, who have renounced him. There is one especially who, attracted at first by this man, has left him with horror."

The person whom Agostino referred to was Miguel Navarro, who had planned to assassinate Ignatius in Paris. In return for money, Navarro, backed by Pedro de Castillo, Francis Muderra, and Barera, another Spaniard, was ready to testify before Conversini, the governor in Rome, that Ignatius had been condemned as a heretic in Alcalá, Paris, and Venice. Thus, people now had doubts about the sincerity of the Jesuits. Ignatius had no alternative; supported by Cardinal de Cupis, head of the Sacred College, he demanded a trial, and quickly proved the falsity of Navarro's accusations. No one could doubt his words the moment he read a letter written by Navarro at the time of his penitence, praising Ignatius for his virtues and faithful adherence to Catholic doctrine.

The case against Ignatius collapsed, especially when the inquisitors, Dr. Ori of Paris, Dr. Figueroa of Alcalá, and Dr. Caspar de Doctis of Venice, who were in Rome, confirmed the innocence of Ignatius and his followers.

Conversini wanted the matter to end there, and he ordered the opposing parties to be silent. But this attitude did not satisfy Ignatius. He had suffered unjust criticism for too long; he was now determined that it should cease for good.

The pope was then at Nice, and when he returned he quickly left the Vatican for his villa at Frascati. Ignatius followed him, explaining that the Jesuits had been slandered for months. They had now been proved innocent, yet Conversini's verdict did not remove all doubt in the people's minds.

Pope Paul recognized the injustices, and the governor was asked to publish a sentence that "not only had no fault been found in these persons, either in law or in fact, but the excellence of their life and doctrine was fully shown; and while their accusers proved to have uttered only false and empty statements, the best men, on the contrary, had given the strongest testimony in their favor."

Retribution eventually came to the accusers. Agostino would die on the order of the Spanish Inquisition. Navarro, penitent once again, sought Ignatius' charity.

Later that year the Company had problems of a different nature. Famine, induced by a severe winter, spread tragedy in Rome. The sick and the starving lay in the streets. Ignatius and his companions moved among them at all times of the day and night, offering whatever relief they could.

The Jesuits' reputation was now so high that wealthy citizens gave them food, clothing, and money to help the poor. In those critical days, more than four hundred people were cared for in the Jesuits' own house, and altogether some three thousand received some form of aid.

It was during that dreadful period—at Christmastime— that Ignatius said the Mass that he had delayed for so long. To his brother he wrote: "I went at Christmas to Santa Maria Maggiore, and said there, with the help and grace of God, my first Mass, in the chapel which contains the crypt where the infant Jesus was laid."

CHAPTER 11

THE COMPANY OF JESUS

Whereas the companions had long been the object of enmity and criticism. They were now so popular that this began to cause problems. They were referred to by the people as the pilgrim priests. Because they had placed themselves at the pope's disposal, it was the practice to give them special assignments in different parts of Europe. This raised their prestige but it disrupted the work of giving the Spiritual Exercises, and the Company itself had no organization. Furthermore, the companions had no official head.

On April 15, 1539, the Jesuits met at night to discuss whether they should try to form an organized community or remain individual missionaries serving the cardinals. If they were organized it was clear that one of them must head the Order. But would they all be willing to obey one of their Company?

It was also explained that the oath of obedience might deter others from joining them. One had also to remember that some ecclesiastical dignitaries objected to the creation of new Orders. In that event, their small Company might cease to exist. Much thought, it was pointed out, should be given to those matters.

The Jesuits gathered to vote on these issues early in May. All were unanimous in seeking the establishment of a new Order. Moreover, it was stressed that everyone who joined the Company must take a vow of obedience to the pope. Other resolutions asserted that they were to choose a superior, whom they must obey for life. Each member should give public instruction in the commandments and catechism, for about one hour each, forty days a year. All recruits must go through the Spiritual Exercises for three months before they were accepted as novices. Finally, the Company's affairs should be decided by a majority vote of the members in Italy. For the moment the membership was to be confined to sixty, but three years later that restriction was withdrawn.

Ignatius, by general consent, had been chosen to formulate the petition for presentation to the pope. The document began: "He who wishes to fight for God under the banner of the Cross and serve Our Lord alone and His Vicar on earth in our Company, which we wish to be marked by the name of Jesus, should keep in mind that, after a vow of chastity, he is a part of a community which has been founded principally for the advancing of souls in Christian life and doctrine, and of spreading the faith by means of the word, *Spiritual Exercises*, works of charity, and especially in the teaching of children and ordinary persons in Christian principles. . . ."

Ignatius found Cardinal Contrarini a keen advocate of the petition. Giving such strong backing, it was appropriate that the cardinal should present it to the pope, who, in turn, asked Tommaso Badia, Master of the Sacred Palace, to comment upon it. Badia soundly recommended it, and on reading the constitutions, Pope Paul remarked: "The finger of God is here."

But opposition was to come. The petition had still to be approved by three cardinals. One of these, Bartolomeo Giudiccioni of Lucca, objected to yet another Order. His opposition was not baseless; in his view far too many Orders already existed and these were far too degenerate. When corruption among these communities was so rife, he argued, why create yet another? A better plan, he suggested, would be to get rid of some.

For months Giudiccioni was so adamant that he stubbornly declined to read the petition. Ignatius resorted to prayer and vowed an offering of three thousand Masses should the negotiations succeed. When finally Giudiccioni relented, the constitutions so impressed him that he readily advised the pope to approve.

On September 27, 1540, a papal bull founded the Order of the Company of Jesus. More than a year had gone by since the petition was first submitted to the pope.

The new Order's name would eventually inspire more criticism. When Cardinal de Cueva called it presumptuous, Ignatius replied: "Let them call us the Congregation or Order of Jesus if they will not call us the Company of Jesus, but I do not think the name of Jesus can ever be taken from us." And later, in 1554, when the Sorbonne also attacked the movement, Miguel de Torres, writing from Spain, claimed that some members of the Society questioned if the name was suitable in view of the jealousy it inspired. Ignatius replied: "The name has a deeper root than the world wits of, and cannot be changed."

The fact that the Jesuits were exempt from singing divine office in choir also annoyed the older Orders.

Now that the Company was a recognized Order, it was imperative to appoint an official head. All the companions who could do so returned to Rome at Easter, 1541. The absentees included Xavier and Rodriguez, who were now in the service of the Portuguese king. Rodriguez was to stay in Portugal, but Xavier left for missionary activities in Goa and the East. Within a decade his preaching would take him from Goa to Japan, where he would accomplish heroic achievements.

Xavier and Rodriguez, aware of the forthcoming election, had left their votes in sealed envelopes before they departed. Other absentees sent theirs in writing—all save Bobadilla, who was working in Naples. His vote, for an unknown reason, was never received.

Actually, only six of the fathers attended the election in Rome. It was no ordinary ballot, for there was a strong religious flavor about it. The voting papers were placed in a box; then for three days the companions engaged in prayer and meditation before the count was taken on April 7.

All the votes, except his own, were in favor of Ignatius. On the papers were written explanatory notes. Codure's was typical: "With no thought but for the greater glory of God and the great glory of the whole Society, I vote for the man who in my judgment ought to be head and minister of the Society. That man—and I bear witness that I have always known him zealous for the honor of God and most ardent

96

for the salvation of souls, and he ought to be set over others for the reason that he has ministered to them and made himself the least among them—is our honored Father, Don Ignatius Loyola; and after him I choose a man not less endowed with virtues, our honored Father Peter Favre. This is the truth before God the Father and Our Lord Jesus Christ; nor should I say otherwise even if I knew for sure that this was the last hour of my life."

Ignatius, however, asked the companions to consider the matter again. But at the second count on April 10 the resolution was the same. Indeed, Laínez refused to accept anyone else as superior, and threatened to quit the Company if Ignatius declined.

Still uncertain as to what he should do, Ignatius finally agreed to leave the decision to his confessor, Father Theodoric, a friar of the Convent of San Pietro in Montorio. For three days, Ignatius confessed and submitted his arguments, but in the end Theodoric advised him to accept. His decision was received by the Society on a sealed sheet of paper.

On April 22, the first Friday after Easter, the Jesuits, who were then in Rome, visited the seven pilgrimage churches before entering St. Paul's-Beyond-the-Walls. At the altar of the Blessed Virgin, Ignatius said Mass. Holding the host, he turned toward his brethren and read this vow of obedience to the Pope: "I, Ignatius Loyola, vow to God Almighty, and to the Supreme Pontiff, His Vicar on earth, in the presence of the Virgin His Mother and of the whole Company of Heaven, and in the presence of the Company, perpetual poverty, chastity and obedience, in accordance with the provisions of the Bull confirming the Company of Our Lord Jesus, and contained in the constitution as drawn

97

or to be drawn. Moreover, I vow obedience in particular to the Supreme Pontiff concerning missions as set forth in the Bull. And I further vow that I will teach boys in the principles of the faith according to the Bull and the constitution." Ignatius then took Holy Communion.

Laínez, Salmerón, Broët, Le Jay, and Codure, kneeling before the altar, vowed obedience to Ignatius and also received Communion. In this simple way, Ignatius was not only the founder, but had become the first general of the Order of the Company of Jesus. He was fifty years old.

Although now the official leader, Ignatius continued to share the humblest duties. One task after his appointment was to work in the kitchen for forty-six days. Speaking in poor Italian, he taught the catechism in a small church that no longer exists. Adults as well as children listened to him.

His life, however, changed in the sense that his wanderings were over. Although the rest of the brethren would travel on missions, Ignatius alone would remain permanently in Rome, the pivotal point of the Jesuit movement. Manifold tasks lay ahead of him, for the missions of the companions and the administration of the Order would increase.

For that reason, in the early days of his generalship Ignatius realized that some assistance was essential. So, when political disturbances prevented Jean Codure from going to Ireland, he became Ignatius' secretary. But within months Codure fell seriously ill, and when he showed no signs of recovering, Ignatius, with two disciples, set off across Rome to say Mass for him at San Pietro in Montorio. On reaching the Sistine Bridge, Ignatius stopped and said: "Let us return. Codure is dead." He was proved to be right.

Ignatius had lost one more of his pioneer members, but recruits were soon to arrive in Rome. Among them were Laínez' brother and two of Ignatius' nephews.

Meanwhile, he had drafted nine provisional rules that the companions must follow until the constitutions—the Society's rules—were completed. The constitutions would be changed from time to time and would not be finalized for some years.

Perhaps influenced by his early life as a soldier, Ignatius put great stress on discipline and obedience. By some standards his orders were excessive, yet he applied the same severities to himself. It was this discipline, furthermore, that was rigorously to withstand the spread of heresy.

It must be remembered that this was an age in which the Catholic Church was beset with many troubles. A weak movement, therefore, could not have helped resolve them.

Ignatius did not expect his disciples to question or try to choose their missions, but to wholeheartedly undertake what was assigned to them. His skill in teaching and his style of training set the hallmark on the Jesuit movement, which gradually developed into a vast army. He was in the habit of asking three questions of the members. Were they willing to obey in whatever occupation he chose for them? Did they think themselves better fitted for one occupation than another? Would they prefer one occupation to another?

In eleven instructions on obedience written by Ignatius, a Jesuit was expected to do the will of his superior in all things except sin. He should also wish to be ruled by a superior who tried to subjugate his judgment and subdue his understanding. In the eighth principle, Ignatius went so far as to claim that the Society "ought to be like a corpse, which has neither will nor understanding; or like a little crucifix which is turned about at the will of him who holds it; or like a staff in the hands of an old man who uses it as may assist or please him. So ought I to be under my religious rule, doing whatever service is judged best."

Under the constitutions, a vow bound a member to the Society for life unless he was dismissed.

Members were separated into different grades. There were lay brothers or coadjutors, both spiritual and temporal. The spiritual element were to help the professed fathers in their ministry, the temporal to be restricted to work in the houses. Next came the scholastics, who were preparing for the priesthood, and then the ordinary fathers. Finally, there were the professed fathers, who were to be the mainstay of the movement and the ones eligible for the highest posts.

From the time that Ignatius and his early disciples first preached in the streets, preaching to the people was a major characteristic of the Society. But it was to go further. It concentrated on teaching the young, and also specialized in influencing the powerful controlling class—for instance, monarchs and the nobility. In that sense, it is unique among religious bodies, and has rightly been described as an aristocratic and intellectual movement among the Orders.

CHAPTER 12

THE GENERAL IN ROME

After Pope Paul III officially recognized the Society, Ignatius had sixteen more years to live. During that time, he saw his organization spread internationally. It would be ever ready to respond to the call of the pontiff, going wherever he requested. Many missions would be undertaken abroad, and the Jesuits would resist, and finally stem, the growing forces of Protestantism that threatened the Church.

Jesuit houses also began to appear in the main cities of Europe. Quite naturally the first was set up in Rome. Of this, Father Pedro de Ribandaneira recorded: "We lived in great poverty and discomfort, and in an old, dilapidated, hired house in front of the old church of the Society; it was later knocked down and its place was taken by the one we now possess."

The house in Rome was close to the Jesuits' own church —Santa Maria della Strada—where the magnificent basilica of the Gesu now stands. At that time there were more than thirty members of the community. The rules were strict. Each officer, from the superior down to the doorkeeper, was entrusted with specific duties. Sleep was limited to seven hours, when a "waker-up" knocked on the bedroom doors. Should anyone still be in bed fifteen minutes later, the waker-up was directed to enter the room and pull the mattress half off the bed. Ignatius insisted on beds being made before sunrise.

Bells announced the times for prayers and meals. It was customary at dinner to read from three books: the Bible, a treatise on contempt for worldly things, and a biography of a saint.

Beside the house was a garden, and the Jesuits also owned a vineyard on the Aventine. Here the novices were allowed to play only piastrella, similar to games played today with rings that are thrown over hooks or pegs. Piastrella had been played at the Sorbonne when Ignatius studied in Paris. He himself made the wax model for the piastrella.

The second Jesuit house was founded in the monastery of St. Anthony in Lisbon, and the third house was opened in Paris. Next, in April, 1542, a little poorhouse was established in Padua, and two months later started the now celebrated college of Coimbra.

In those sixteen years the Society grew to the extent that Ignatius' secretary at the time, Father Juan Polanco, writing six days after the founder's death, recorded: "Our Father, between 1540, when the Society was confirmed, and the present day, had established twelve well-organized provinces; or thirteen, if we include Ethiopia, where Father Tibertius or Anthony de Cuadros was Provincial. There in Flanders they have news of six, viz. of the Indies, Brazil, Portugal, Andalucia, Castile, and Aragon; in Sicily, Master Jerome Domenech is Provincial; in Italy, outside Rome,

Master Laínez. In Rome, Naples, and Tivoli there is no Provincial, as all this region can conveniently be governed by the General. In France, the Provincial is Master Pascasio (Broët); in Flanders, Master Bernard Oliviero, and in Germany, Dr. Canisius. The colleges and houses opened during the lifetime of our Father number more than a hundred."

As the Society developed, each country was split up into one or more provinces. At the head of each Ignatius appointed a superior called a provincial. Every provincial was expected to write to Ignatius regularly in detail on matters pertaining to his province. Even the attitude of influential people, such as princes and bishops, was noted.

The creation and structure of the Society greatly reflected Ignatius' own personality. The onetime soldier infused a military discipline into his brethren. He was both kind and stern. He would tend the sick in hospitals at night and would write solicitous letters to any father who was ill. Yet so keenly did he instill poverty into the Jesuits that he was angry with anyone who dared to pick even a solitary flower. In the garden no one was permitted to eat or touch grapes or other fruit without permission.

The rules also reveal Ignatius as a stickler for detail. They dealt with so many points that no one could misunderstand his commands. For instance, piastrella could not be played on the little paths that ran across the width of the vineyard. Neither the players nor anyone else were allowed to lean against the trelliswork. No one was to break twigs from the trees or vines, or make marks on them. Every player was to be careful to return the piastrella he had played with to the gate of the house and hand it to the moni-

103

tor. The latter was to ensure that the correct number had been returned to him and put in the closet appropriated for the purpose.

Ignatius was equally exacting with himself, and each day was one of rigid routine. Every morning began with an hour's meditation, followed by Mass, to which he usually devoted another hour. He did not, however, expect other priests to take so much time; half an hour was quite sufficient. Next came two hours of prayer. Ignatius was in the habit of kneeling beside a little window in his room, from which he saw the Church of Santa Maria della Strada. His prayers ended, visitors—no one, no matter how humble, was barred—were received. Should there be no visitors, he usually left the house on business or called on the sick and poor in the company of a companion.

The midday meal was taken in the refectory with the brethren. With Ignatius sat his earliest disciples and guests. Father Benedetto Palmio once wrote: "His table was always resplendent with parsimony and frugality, but it had nevertheless a savor of gentle usages. There were two or three brothers to wait upon it, more especially when outsiders were invited to dinner. The wineglasses were served with elegance; it could not have been better done, or more attractively, in a palace."

After the meal they all retired to a room allocated for recreation and discussion. An hourglass indicated when it was time for Ignatius to leave to write letters or dictate them to a secretary. After supper those entrusted with duties in the house reported to him and received instructions. This completed, he discussed the Society's affairs with his secretary and was then left alone in his room for meditation and prayer. Ignatius never retired until late; he limited his sleeping to four hours.

This daily routine mirrored Ignatius' character. He was a man of simple tastes and of a quite serious nature. He bore the manner and displayed the courtesy of the aristocrat. He was not an eloquent, but a persuasive speaker. He preferred to listen rather than talk. Indeed, he did not read or write his native language very well. And one can appreciate the many inaccuracies when he preached in Italian. Yet no one could mistake the sincerity in his voice.

A keen adherent of the Jesuit rules, he expected others to be the same. When a father erred, no matter how slightly, Ignatius could be forthright and austere. He did not like any of his brethren to show self-interest. When, for instance, Bobadilla tried to get a bigger room for himself, he was ordered to accommodate two more companions with him. And when novices were clearly ill-suited to the Order, Ignatius quickly dismissed them. There was no hesitation; he promptly told them to go, and after such dismissals he was extremely cheerful. On one occasion as many as nine were ordered to leave. Later ten more were dismissed.

Idleness angered Ignatius enormously. When he asked a lay brother for whom he was working, the brother replied: "For God and His love." "Then," said Ignatius, "I assure you if you do no better henceforth I shall penance you soundly. Were you working for me, it might be no great matter to take so small trouble over it; but to work thus carelessly for God holds no excuse."

Father Ribadaneira described Ignatius as being "of medium height, or, more accurately, somewhat below the average, with a small frame, although his brothers were tall, and well formed. His countenance commanded respect, his forehead was high and without wrinkles, his eyes deep-set, the eyelids puckered and wrinkled with his many tears, the ears of medium size, the nose high and curved, a somewhat ruddy complexion, his head bald, and his whole aspect venerable. His appearance was joyfully grave and gravely joyful, so that his serenity rejoiced those who looked on him, while his gravity impressed all about him."

Direct and to the point in speech, Ignatius expected others to be the same. Probably this tended to overstress his austerity, for basically Ignatius was very kind and humble. Whatever treatment he meted out to others was essentially for the good of that person; for example, there was a lazy novice who neglected his room. Ignatius commanded him to put some of the articles in the room into a sack, then carry it around the house declaring his slovenliness.

Curiously, although Ignatius was almost obsessed with cleanliness himself, he seems to have discouraged novices to be likewise. In his autobiography Father Benedetto Palmiro, who first worked in the kitchen on entering the Roman community, reveals (writing in the third person): "Benedetto . . . felt great disgust at the dirt in the kitchen and dining hall. At this time there were two causes that contributed largely to make the house dirty: great scarcity and the class of novices that attended to the household chores—for they took little or no pains in the matter of personal cleanliness. The consequence was that Benedetto could not look at the horrid, dirty place, where he was at work, without being sick at his stomach. . . . At last he hit upon a plan for getting over his disgust and squeamishness. . . . Under the kitchen was a cellar filled with filth;

down into this cellar Benedetto went, rolled in the filth, and covered himself with it from head to foot, and in this guise went about the house in triumphant joy. . . .

"When Ignatius saw him all covered with filth, he used these words: 'Now at last you please me, Benedetto.' "

In a novice, Ignatius could tolerate dirt but not conceit. Thus, an arrogant novice was made to wear wings before others in the refectory while a colleague lectured him on attempting to fly before his wings were fully grown. Ignatius was also known to draw a circle around a novice who had done wrong, forcing him to stay there until he allowed him to leave. Any offender met with rebuke.

It must not be imagined that, because of his insistence on discipline, Ignatius was a dictator. He was willing to listen to the opinions of others, and even accept advice. He openly admitted that "there was not in all the house one who did not in some thing give him an example to meditate or some cause to humble himself by comparison."

This readiness to receive other views was allied with his refusal to reach a decision quickly. He preferred to consider all aspects first. Perhaps his outstanding traits were his magnetic personality and his remarkable gift of friendship. Before the latter, indignation and anger could quickly melt away.

Such was the case with Miguel Torres, the rector of the University of Alcalá, who was hostile to the Jesuits. On a visit to Rome the ambassador suggested that he should meet Salmerón. But at first he stubbornly refused. Eventually, Torres yielded and met him secretly. When Salmerón proposed a meeting with Ignatius, Torres indignantly replied: "Do you suppose I would speak to such a man?" But again

107

he gave in. It was arranged that he should meet Ignatius in the garden of the Jesuit house. Ignatius' charm so disarmed the rector that, as if in despair, Torres cried: "Do with me what you please."

After making the Spiritual Exercises, Torres quit the worldliness of the university, and Ignatius appointed him rector of the Jesuit College at Salamanca.

CHAPTER 13

LEADER OF MISSIONARIES

At one time Ignatius had ambitions to be a missionary, taking the Scriptures to the infidel. Instead, he became the leader of missionaries, ruling and inspiring them from Rome. Indeed, on only three occasions did he interrupt his administrative tasks and leave the city.

The first occasion was to talk with Paul III at Moneofiascone, in regard to the Portuguese Inquisition. The second was to prevent blood-spilling in a quarrel between the peoples of Tivoli and San Angelo. His third journey was to Alirto in Naples to effect a reunion—which turned out to be only temporary—between the influential Ascano Colonna and his wife, Joanna of Aragon. Incidentally, at that time it rained with such force that Polanco, who accompanied Ignatius, pleaded to put off their journey. Ignatius refused. "It is thirty years since I put off anything I undertook in God's service, happen what might," he replied.

Other than these trips, it was necessary for Ignatius to remain in Rome to direct the growing activities of his Order. There were the spiritual assaults in the form of missions. In explaining the vow of obedience to the pope, Ignatius had written: "To whatever part of the world the Supreme Pontiff desires to send us, we on our part are obliged to obey instantly . . . without excuse, whether they send us to the Turks or to any infidels, even to those who dwell in the regions called the Indies, or to heretics or schismatics, or anywhere among the faithful."

In the case of the latter, there was the mission to Ireland. Codure had been chosen to go, but after his death Broët took his place and was accompanied by Salmerón. A young nobleman, Francisco Zapata, joined them. Keen to enter the Society, he financed the mission and began his novitiate.

The reason for the journey was the English Reformation. Henry VIII had cast off all allegiance to the pope, and with Thomas Cromwell, his minister, the king was trying to force the Irish to recognize him as the supreme religious head. The priests who refused to submit had fled or were in hiding. Robert Wauchop, the blind primate of Ireland and archbishop of Armagh, pleaded with the pope to send an apostolic nuncio to help to raise the morale of the downtrodden people.

Before Broët and his colleagues left, Ignatius schooled them in the way they should approach people who might ease their task. It reveals to some degree the subtle way in which he influenced others. He advised: "In order to make acquaintance with great persons . . . first study their character, and act accordingly. If, for example, a man be of a hasty temper and speaks rapidly and much, then assume with him something of a familiar tone, adopt his way, but let it be about things good and holy, and be not too serious, or reserved, or melancholy. But with those of a more phlegmatic character, who are slow of speech, grave and measured in discourse, adopt a manner similar to theirs; this is sure to propitiate them. 'I make myself all things to all men.' "

First the three men journeyed to Scotland where, at Stirling Castle, the Scottish monarch assured the papal representatives of his loyalty. They landed in Ireland during the Lenten season, 1542, wearing disguises to lessen the danger of detection. But their plans were no longer secret. Somehow the viceroy had learned of their intentions, and offered a reward for their capture. Anyone who harbored them faced possible death. The Irish lived in a state of fear, and although the small party traveled secretly throughout the country for thirty-four days, there was little they could do, Therefore, they journeyed to Paris, where the pope, on being told of the terrorism in Ireland, ordered Broët and Salmerón to return to Rome.

Zapata stayed on in Paris to study before going to Italy for his novitiate. Foolishly he made the mistake of unjustifiably scoffing at Nadal for preaching to charlatans. Ignatius roused him from his bed, ordering him to leave the Society in the morning.

Francis Xavier was to be the most conspicuous of the religious adventurers. His preaching in the East would echo throughout Christian countries. Embarking at Lisbon on April 7, 1541, he endured the tedium and the hazards of a thirteen-month-long voyage, reaching Goa on May 6, 1542. Following the Jesuit pattern, he first taught the Catechism to children and preached in the prisons and the hospitals. By October he was preaching the Gospel on the Fishery Coast.

111

From there Xavier sent his famous letter, dated January 12, 1544, to Ignatius. It was the first description of Jesuit missionary fervency to reach Rome. Translated into Latin, it went from country to country throughout Christendom, drawing many to the Society.

Father Antonio de Araoz, Ignatius' nephew, recorded that Cardinal Tavera, archbishop of Toledo, "had the whole letter of our brother, Master F. Xavier, read to him, and was much pleased with it, as have many in those parts, so that he has reaped no less pleasure in Spain and Portugal with his letter than he has in the Indies with his teaching." (Incidentally, it was Ignatius' practice on receiving letters that were highly favorable to the Society to have them distributed, especially to people of influence and power.)

In his incredible way, Xavier—during 1542—spread knowledge of the Gospel along India's west coast, from Goa to Cape Comorin, then into Ceylon and east of India. His travels took him to Malacca, a busy Portuguese market, and to the islands of Moro.

Back at Malacca he greeted a party of missionaries from Portugal. These people enabled him to found Jesuit houses in such places as Goa, Malacca, Cochin, and Ternate.

In 1549 Xavier began to evangelize Japan, suffering acute privations in the process. He left Christian missions in his wake, but Ignatius wanted to set up Jesuit houses there, too. And so he sent Xavier a letter on June 20, 1553, asking him to return to Rome and discuss the matter.

The letter, which still survives, gave rise to a false rumor among Jesuits. People thought that Ignatius intended to appoint Xavier as his successor. But Ignatius was merely seeking a full account of the territories so that he could extend Gospel teaching. In any event, the letter was sent too late. No doubt enfeebled by his enormous tasks, Xavier had died in December, 1552.

Meanwhile, the Jesuits were also active in Africa. An expedition to the Congo—led by Diego Diaz, Christobal Ribeiro, and Jorge Alvarez, with a coadjutor, Diego Loveral —took place at the end of 1547. The men did not reach their goal until early in the following year.

The king of the Congo and the Portuguese cooperated with the Jesuits and provided interpreters. Thus, the Jesuits conveyed the Gospel to the natives, many of whom were drawn to the Christian faith. The mission, however, was only temporary. The language barrier was not the Jesuits' sole handicap; there were also the harsh rigors of the climate, which undermined their health.

This exacting life seriously affected other Jesuits when they arrived at Tetuan to try to release slaves. A number of slaves were rescued in prison and others were helped by alms, but again no permanent mission was founded.

For many years, despite other expeditions, the Jesuits had no definite home in Africa. How different from the missionary work in Japan and Brazil! Juan de Azpilcueta, from Navarre, sailed from Lisbon on February 1, 1549. Fifty-six days elapsed before he landed in South America.

Heartbreaking tasks lay ahead among the Indians who gathered in the vicinity of Portuguese settlements. Curiously, according to Father Polanco, Azpilcueta was able to overcome the language problem. If a record left by Ignatius' secretary is accurate, Azpilcueta mastered the language within a matter of days simply because it was similar to his native Basque. If that is so, it must have been a valuable tool in helping to eradicate such practices as cannibalism, which was common among the Indians. The mission grew so fast that other missions had to be sent from Portugal. In 1553 Ignatius was able to found a province in Brazil.

Nothing gave Ignatius greater satisfaction than to increase the tempo in the mission field. In 1554 he complied with a request from King John III of Portugal to send an expedition to Ethiopia. With a party of twelve missionaries, the expedition was unique in that the three chief members had been elevated to the rank of bishop. Father Juan Nunez Barreto, a Portuguese, was both superior and patriarch of Ethiopia. He was accompanied by Father Andres de Oviedo, bishop of Hierapolis, and Father Melchior Carnero, bishop of Nicea. But the expedition did not leave Portugal until 1555. Ignatius never learned of the mission's progress, for by the time it began to establish itself, he was dead.

Ignatius himself never stifled his early desire to preach to the infidel. Although in poor health, and while the Ethiopian adventure was being organized, he was anxious to lead a mission to Tripoli and Tunis. But this plan never matured in his lifetime, nor did he fulfill a request to send Jesuits to the Spanish Indies. However, this would be accomplished by a successor, Francis Borgia, the man who had once passed Ignatius in a street in Alcalá while the Jesuit was on his way to prison. Borgia founded the province of Peru in 1556, and that of Mexico sixteen years later.

114

CHAPTER 14

CAMPAIGN AGAINST HERESY

The wording of the Jesuit vow of obedience to the pope—especially the reference to heresy—virtually guaranteed that the Society would be employed in countering Protestantism, which had spread in northern Europe, France, Spain and elsewhere. This great religious controversy, which fomented such strife in the Catholic Church, was set off by Martin Luther, an Augustinian monk.

In 1511 Luther had gone to Rome as a pilgrim and, in a sense, returned a Protestant. A theologian of tremendous eloquence, to whom crowds thronged to hear preach, he was horrified by the decadence that he had witnessed in the Eternal City.

On returning to the University of Wittenberg, where he was a professor, Luther had the degree of doctor of divinity bestowed on him. Pointing somewhat to coming events, the oath that he took at the time was "to devote his whole life to study, and faithfully to expound and defend the Holy Scriptures."

The Reformation was born in 1517. At the request of Leo X, the new pontiff, agents moved about Germany selling what were known as indulgences—penances to receive God's blessing. Luther was appalled, realizing that God's forgiveness could not be bought for money. When John Tetzel, one of the papal agents, came to Saxony, Luther bitterly attacked him from the Wittenberg pulpit. He also wrote to princes and bishops pleading with them to debar these religious peddlers.

But Tetzel went unimpeded. When, however, he got to Jüteborg, near Wittenberg, Luther could contain himself no longer. Writing ninety-five theses denouncing indulgences, he nailed the paper to the door of the castle church on All Saints' Day, October 31, 1517.

Very soon the hammering on that door reverberated throughout Germany. Luther heatedly harangued the practice of pardon-selling, but he did not condemn indulgences entirely. Yet in his theses and sermons on the subject, he insisted that true repentance comprised three ingredients: contrition, confession, and absolution. Heartfelt sorrow for sin was, in Luther's view, the thing that mattered.

Pilgrims who came to Wittenberg to buy the indulgences went away without them. Instead, they left with the unforgettable words of Luther's sermons. He influenced not only ordinary folk but many princes, bishops, and monks. Indeed, numerous Germans were outraged. The significant effect of all this was that Luther was undermining traditional ecclesiastical practice.

The Church, for instance, contended that the individual must confess his sins to God through the medium of the priest. And pardon, it was claimed, was achieved only by means of the priest's absolution. Luther now argued that in seeking forgiveness of sin, the individual could go straight to God without the aid of anyone else.

The word "spiritual," in Luther's opinion, had become abused and misused. As used by the Church it did not refer so much to inward religious experience. A person, for example, was "spiritual" if he had been ordained a priest. Any gift was also "spiritual" if it was donated to the Church. The description, owing to misuse, was no better than a commercial label.

In May, 1518, Luther wrote to some of the German bishops and urged reform of the Church. His action stirred others to oppose him, the most forceful being John Eck, a former fellow student, at Ingolstadt. Eck denounced Luther as a heretic. Not unexpectedly, Luther was summoned to appear before the pope in Rome. But the Elector of Saxony intervened, and the rebel monk was allowed to present himself to the pope's legate at Augsburg.

By now Luther had such overwhelming support in Germany that the pope told the cardinal legate, James de Vio of Gaeta—more usually known as Cajetan—to be conciliatory. But Cajetan so attacked Luther that, fearing he would be seized, he left Augsburg secretly. The outcome of the meeting disturbed the Elector. Luther offered to leave Saxony, but was allowed to remain.

The pope now sent another legate to speak with Luther. His name was Carl von Militz, and he saw Luther privately in the house of Spalatin, court preacher to the Elector. This discussion was more amicable. Luther agreed to apologize in writing to the pope, and he promised to refrain from further controversy, provided his adversaries did likewise.

Eck, however, again resumed the dispute and Luther retaliated. Among other things, he contended that although the Church could dispense with the pope, the pope had need of the Church. The papacy, he challenged, had placed the Catholic Church in bondage. Luther also opposed the sending of money annually from Germany to the Vatican. "Why," he argued, "should 300,000 florins be sent every year from Germany to Rome?"

When Luther refused to recant, excommunication was inevitable. On July 15, 1520, a papal bull condemned Martin Luther for heresy, but when copies were posted in German towns, most of them were torn down by the people. The final insult to Rome occurred on December 10. Luther led a procession of professors and students to the marketplace and threw the bull into a fire.

Germany would no longer be ruled by the law of the pope, but by the law of the land. It was the renunciation in Germany of the medieval doctrine that emanated from Rome.

But the Reformation was more than that; it was the outcome of years of religious discontent in Europe generally— a slow festering of revolt that had begun even before Ignatius was born. Sovereigns had smarted under the interference of popes in secular affairs. Kings and their peoples had smoldered owing to the need to subscribe to the papal treasury in such ways as tithes and annuities. Seemingly more interested in materialism than piety, some pontiffs had closed their eyes to corruption in the Catholic Church. Luther's action, therefore, fired the charge that caused the religious explosion.

For political reasons, Emperor Charles V was anxious to

restore religious unity in Germany to withstand a growing threat from the Turks. Thus, wishing to end this religious quarrel, in 1520 he convened a diet, which assembled at Worms. This was the year before Ignatius was appointed general, and it was proof of the growing importance of the Jesuits that Charles requested the pope and Ignatius to choose someone of great moral integrity and eloquence to speak for the Catholic cause.

Favre was the Jesuit who was chosen, and his letters to Ignatius clearly reveal that it was not merely Lutheranism that was undermining papal authority; there was also depressing decadence among the clergy. On New Year's Day, 1541, he wrote:

> I wonder there are not twice or three times the number of heretics as there are, because nothing leads to errors in belief so rapidly as a disordered life. It is not the false interpretations of Scripture, nor the sophistry which the Lutherans introduce into their sermons and disputes that have caused so many countries to apostatize and so many towns and provinces to revolt against religion. All the mischief is done by the scandalous lives of the clergy. Would there were in this city of Worms at least two or three churchmen who were not living openly in sin or guilty of some other notorious crime, but who had a little zeal for the salvation of souls. They might do anything they pleased with these simple people; I mean in the towns where they have now abolished all the laws and practices of religion, and entirely free from obedience to the apostolic see. But that part of the flock which is bound to lead the

faithless into the fold is precisely that which drives Catholics to become Lutherans by the spectacle of their dissolute lives.

Of all the clergy in Worms, Favre came across only one priest whose morals were beyond reproach. Between them they managed to prevent a complete abandonment of the faith from sweeping the town.

Favre, however, failed to bridge the gap between Catholics and Lutherans. Indeed, the whole of Jesuit pressures that were to follow would never be enough to bring Luther back within the Church. The fracture was too great and the doctrinal differences too acute. The Protestant Reformation was too strongly identified with the trend that led from the medieval to the modern era in European history.

Instead of healing the wounds, Catholics and Protestants would gradually strive to bring about the other's destruction. However, to Favre and his Jesuit successors in Germany would be attributed much of the credit for eventually containing the Reformation. Europe was then composed of many states, and in the end the Reformation would be restricted to the north.

The discussion at Worms ended in a failure to reach any agreement, but the following year another conference was convened in Ratisbon and attended by the emperor himself. Charles was still keen to effect unity in Germany. Not that he had any serious religious motives; his interest was primarily political because of the threat not only from Turkey but also now from France.

Both religious parties were presented on this second occasion by more moderate spokesmen, yet unity was still

120

evasive, partly due to the intrigues of Charles' rival, Francis of France. Favre, on his part, was not interested in political scheming. He was solely concerned with supporting the Catholic cause on behalf of the pope and improving moral standards in the Church. Even so, conciliation was never secured.

Le Jay and Bobadilla temporarily replaced Favre when the pope and Ignatius ordered him to accompany Ortiz on a mission to Spain. The first to arrive in Germany was Le Jay, who had to speak Latin or French because he knew no German. This handicap was bad enough, but Le Jay also got no help from the clergy. Their silence implied that they favored the Lutherans. And when he attempted to reform the priests, he merely roused their hostility.

Moreover, Le Jay so angered the people by his attacks on heresy that once they threatened to throw him into the Danube. Fearlessly, he countered with the remark: "What does it matter to me whether I enter Heaven from earth or water?"

Le Jay must have derived some comfort when he was eventually joined by Bobadilla, who had journeyed somewhat leisurely. In Vienna he, too, had found degeneracy among the priests, who were indifferent to the people.

After two years of struggle in Ratisbon, Le Jay went on Ignatius' instructions to Ingolstadt. There he was more successful in combating the Reformation by winning the Duke of Bavaria's support. "Sooner would I forfeit my kingdom," the duke declared, "than give up a man of mine to Luther."

From Ingolstadt, Le Jay took his religious campaign to Dillingen, then on to Salzburg. There, at a gathering of the opposing factions, he countered a Lutheran demand for a national council. But the bishops induced Le Jay to urge Pope Paul to convene a general council, which had already been promised.

Favre, in the meantime, was experiencing adventures in Spain. Caught up in the war fought by Francis of France and the emperor Charles, Favre was confined to a cell by the French in the castle at Mantua. But by converting his jailer and the commanding officer, he was able to leave to preach and catechize in Spanish towns. In so doing he attracted new recruits to the Society.

While returning to Germany for a further attack on the Lutherans, Favre came close to being captured by brigands on the Spanish frontier and by Lutheran troops on nearing Germany. After he arrived in Germany in October, 1542, he started his preaching campaign at Speyer. From there he went from town to town impressing large crowds by his eloquence. Some who heard him sought to enlist in the Society.

Such a person was the Dutchman Peter Canisius. At the beginning of 1543, Favre was sent to Mainz by the archbishop, Albert of Brandenburg. When twenty-three-year-old Canisius heard Favre preach, he remarked: "Never have I known or listened to a more learned man or one of more eminent virtue—if, indeed, he be a man and not rather an angel from heaven."

Canisius was born at Nimeguen in the year when Ignatius was seriously hurt at Pamplona. The son of rich parents, he was a doctor of philosophy when nineteen years old. His father was the governor to the sons of the Duke of Lorraine. In infancy it had been predicted that Peter would become a member of a movement called the Society of Jesus.

This graduate of the universities of Cologne and Louvain went with Favre to Cologne, where he learned that his father was critically ill. He reached Holland just before his father died. That night he was convinced that in a vision he gained assurance that his father and mother, who was also dead, were certain of salvation. In gratitude, he unhesitatingly gave his huge inheritance to the poor and, returning to Favre, gained admission to the Society.

In Cologne, where Tyndale had printed the Bible, Favre renewed the struggle with the Lutherans. At the request of Spanish Catholics he found himself opposing Archbishop Hermann von Wied, a German prince, who the Emperor Charles had said was "so ignorant that he could not even say Mass." Von Wied knew no Latin, could not read the Introit, and wore secular clothes. And like the German princes generally, he was drawn to Protestantism. Gropper, the archdeacon, failed to have any influence on von Wied, and in desperation the Catholics appealed to Favre.

After a talk, von Wied promised that he would not disobey the pope. Favre was unable to pursue the matter further, for Ignatius instructed him to leave Germany and accompany the daughter of the Portuguese king to Castile, where she was to be the bride of Philip of Spain.

Favre, however, traveled only as far as the Jesuit college at Louvain, where he fell sick. He returned to Germany in January, 1544, but not before he had gathered recruits for the Jesuit college at Coimbra.

In Cologne once more, Favre discovered to his dismay that von Wied had not only broken his promise, but was allowing three prominent Lutherans—Bucer, Pistorius, and Melanchthon—to preach freely. Favre at once plunged into the ecclesiastical fray, so brilliantly opposing the Lutherans in public controversy that citizens besought the emperor to oust the Protestant preachers. The fate of von Wied was excommunication. His inglorious career soon afterward ended in death.

A man of immense humility, Favre briefed his colleagues on the way they should oppose their Lutheran opponents. In a communication to Laínez, he wrote:

All who desire to do them good should show them the greatest charity, love them truly, and disperse all prejudices that might lower us in their esteem. We should seek their goodwill and confidence by a friendly intercourse, conversing of the matters on which we are agreed, and shunning altercation. We should teach them first what they should practice, then what they should believe; not as was the custom of the early Church in those times when men's minds were first of all to receive the faith which comes from hearing and then be led by degrees to the practice of good works. Therefore, we should endeavor to win them from evil ways before we attack their evil doctrine. If Luther himself could be brought to a virtuous life, it would be easy to draw him back into the true Church.

When Ignatius had asked Favre to leave for Spain, Le Jay was entrusted with leading the counterreformation in Germany. Le Jay did not show the same tolerance as Favre and prevailed on the emperor to be more harsh with the Protestants. The new policy rebounded on Canisius and other Jesuits in Cologne. Claiming that their Order was new and not allowed by law, the magistrates ordered their house to be closed.

The Carthusian Order came to the Jesuits' aid, offering them facilities in their own premises. This generous act was to enable Canisius to continue his labors. Years later, when these troubled times were seen in perspective, Canisius would loom as the foremost stalwart of the Catholic Church in the struggle with Protestantism.

As the provincial in Germany, Canisius would be the hub from which the Catholic movement would radiate in northern Europe. Whereas Xavier would be identified with mission work among the infidels, Canisius' name would be deeply etched on the Reformation. His presence in Cologne was part of Ignatius' master plan to dominate in key centers. In four of these he founded teaching colleges: in Cologne, a see of tremendous influence; in Prague, the capital of Bohemia; at Ingolstadt, a university town in Bavaria; and in Vienna. From these four cities Jesuit power spread throughout Germany. There, in the next few years, rose more colleges and universities, which quickly rivaled their Protestant counterparts.

CHAPTER 15

THE COUNCIL OF TRENT

All during this time, both Catholics and Lutherans persisted in their demands for a council, which they had been asking for ever since the outbreak of the Reformation. One reason for the delay was that in Rome—although it was appreciated that there was need for reform in the Church—it was feared that the emperor might use such an assembly for personal gain. There was the risk, for instance, that he might yield in some way to the Lutherans to achieve political stability in his empire. Added to this was the danger that the council might override the pope and introduce reforms that were not only contrary to his wishes, but which seriously undermined his authority. For some time, therefore, the assembly was delayed.

Eventually, the pope and the emperor agreed that a council should be summoned at Trent, a little town in northern Italy, in November, 1542. For various reasons—war among them—there were adjournments until 1546.

From the outset, conflict arose over the interpretation of what was meant by reform. Very broadly, the Catholics wanted a reform of morals; that is, to get rid of abuses in ecclesiastical government and among the priesthood. Whatever concessions they would agree to were restricted to an attempt to restore peace among the parties.

The Lutherans, in contrast, insisted that debates must be based on matters of doctrine.

The council was intended to function as an instrument that would bring about amity between the religious factions. Yet, with the passage of time the deliberations created a widening chasm between Protestant and Catholic.

The Council of Trent—an august assembly embracing the most powerful and influential interests in Europe—was also notable in that it set the seal on the strength of the Jesuit movement. This was amazing, considering that the Order was young and its members relatively few in number.

Although its voice was the most forceful of all in debate, as a movement the Society of Jesus had no place in the Council. Its humble members, wearing patched clothes, were lacking in ecclesiastical dignitaries, yet they derived their authority by attending as representatives of others.

Laínez and Salmerón traveled from Italy as theologians of Pope Paul. They were to have been joined by Favre, but he died on the way from Spain. Le Jay came from Germany and spoke on behalf of Otto Truchses, the cardinal-archbishop of Augsburg. The Duke of Bavaria chose Jean Cuvillon as his representative, and eventually Peter Canisius journeyed from Cologne, briefed by the prince-bishop.

In their unique role, these men—and Laínez in particular—set the pattern of the counterreformation under Ignatius' direction. Ignatius had counseled Laínez and Salmerón on how they should conduct themselves. Although one might have expected a more militant approach in view of the advance of Lutheranism, instead Ignatius advised them to be "slow, rather than prompt, in speaking, considerate and charitable in your opinions of what is done or intended, attentive and calm in listening, taking pains to seize the spirit, desires and intentions of those who speak, so that you may better see when to speak or be silent. In the matters which will be discussed you must state the reasons on both sides so as not to appear attached to your own opinion. You must always . . . contrive that no one shall be less disposed to peace after hearing your discourses than he was before. If the points controverted are such as oblige you to speak, express your opinions modestly and calmly; conclude always 'with deference to better judgments' or some such phrase. Lastly, be well persuaded of this, that to treat worthily of really important subjects, whether human or divine, it is very necessary to discuss them with composure and deliberation, not in haste or in a cursory manner. You should therefore not make the order and time of the discussion suit your leisure and convenience but accommodate the person who wishes to argue with you so that he may the more easily be guided whither God would lead him."

Despite the importance of their discussions in the Council, Laínez, Salmerón, and the other Jesuits were not to neglect their normal duties of hearing confessions, preaching, giving the Exercises, instructing children, and visiting the poor in hospitals. In their sermons they were to avoid the points controverted by the heretics, but to aim always at moral reform and enforce obedience to the Catholic Church.

Laínez and Salmerón spoke with such humility and brilliance that it inspired the bishop of Modena to comment:

129

"The Fathers Laínez and Salmerón have splendidly supported our side against the Protestants respecting the Eucharist. I think myself fortunate in living in an age when I can see and hear these Fathers who are as learned as they are good."

So impressive was Laínez that when he fell victim to bouts of fever, the Council postponed discussion on major issues until he could attend. When Ignatius proposed to transfer Laínez to Florence, he was told that Laínez was irreplaceable.

The conditions, however, under which these Jesuits were first expected to lodge were quite out of keeping with their importance in the assembly. A lengthy letter written by Laínez to Ignatius conveys some idea of the discomfort that Jesuits were willing to tolerate. It also affords some insight into the disposition of Laínez, who would succeed Ignatius as general. Laínez humorously revealed:

> The Secretary [of the Council] took us to his own house and said that, as we were not lodged at an inn, we should come there for just that one night; and he gave us all three, for our joint apartment, a little, tiny, smoky oven of a room with a bed in it and trucklebed (which when pulled out did not leave space to take two steps in the room). There was no table for us to study at, or write a letter, and as for chairs only one footstool, but there were lots of books, belonging to him and his valet, and a big wallet, an old harp and the valet's sword which were kept in our oven.
>
> I said to Master Salmerón, "See here, this is a little more than we bargained for; let's stay at the inn and

tomorrow on my way to the palace I will tell the Secretary that, in order not to go changing inns and as long as he said we were to be here only for one night, we had decided to stay at the inn." But Salmerón thought it was better to come to the oven in spite of the heat in order not to show any signs of discontent with the room or any dissatisfaction. So Salmerón slept that night upon a chest, and John and I upon the beds; but the next day Salmerón betook himself to the house of the Bishop of Verona, which was nearby, to sleep, but though I was offered the same, in order that we should not all leave the apartment, John and I continued to sleep in the oven.

One day the legate's secretary came and asked if we lacked anything: and I answered with my usual freedom or foolishness, "You can see we lack everything." And he said, "That's so, but at the present moment what do you need?" So I answered, "At least we need a candle to go to bed by." Then he asked, "What more?" And I said, laughing all the time, "A candlestick to put it in." However, the keeper of the storecloset was out, so we couldn't have a candle that night; nevertheless, we were the gainers, for we got a torch to go to bed by.

After about a week, having paid visits upon almost everybody, we went to the cardinal to beg him to give us a room; for everybody was asking us where we lodged, and a good many people wanted to come and see us, but we did not think that we could receive visitors where we were. He told us that they would surely give us a room; however, the owner of the house

131

where he wished to lodge us was away, but that, as soon as he came back, he would take us in. The owner did return in three or four days and offered us rooms; but, as the house was new and still unfinished, and as there were neither doors nor windows, he asked for an advance of ten ducats on the rent in order to complete the rooms.

When we went to ask the Secretary of the Council for the ducats . . . the Secretary answered sharply, that he was a dreadful man, etc. After the landlord had gone I said to the Secretary, "It would have been a good thing if you had given him those ducats for in the end they come out of the rent and it makes little difference." To which he said: "What rent do you think that we shall have to pay for those rooms per month, anyhow, that you increase the cost that we shall have to bear in hiring them?" I answered a little indignantly, "Well, there is some expense for every-one that comes to the Council; do you think you spend much for us? Don't you know that we don't eat our bread for nothing, but that we work as hard as the others? The Pope knows that, and that is why he sent us; and you have done a thing that has neither head or tail, in putting two priests, sent by the Pope, into your servant's room, and such a room, that I am aston-ished at you. And since you are not spending your own money you ought to spend according to the orders you receive from the Pope and not keep us all the time where you do; Salmerón had to sleep on a chest the first night and hasn't been willing to sleep there again; and I should have liked to do the same if it had not been that I didn't want to show your short-comings. But I promise you I shall tell the Cardinal how we are situated, and that I shall write it to Rome."

That's the whole story and the full extent of my temper. The good man was scandalized, and (so I have heard) told the Cardinal; and I, quite without anger, rather to please Master Angelo, Secretary of the Council, and the Cardinal, told the Cardinal after supper, laughing in the presence of Master Angelo at all that had passed. I didn't blame Master Angelo but rather my own bad temper and freedom, although at the time it seemed to be right, and seems to me so now, that's why I told the Cardinal.

His Reverence, forewarned by Master Angelo, said that our having no rooms was from no lack of good-will on his part but because of the chance absence of the houseowner; and he excused Master Angelo, saying that as we were in the habit of preaching patience we must also practice it. And I told him truthfully that I had not done this in order to escape discomfort, for the year before I had passed three months in Africa under a sheet, suffering from heat by day and from cold by night, and that in the oven I could laugh and be content, but that I had spoken out because it was not fit and proper for us to have no convenience for study, whether to prepare to preach, to read or anything else, nor towards those that sent us, nor towards his eminence, nor for any members of the Council who might wish to come and see us. . . . And next day, seeing that the matter of the house dragged, for the owner had gone away again and the greater part of it was full of the Cardinal's retinue and there was no place for religious services, and it was expensive for Master Angelo, we went to see our old host of last time and got from him the same rooms we had had before, for so much a month, and he did it most willingly, offering them to us at once and, as he needs the money and gives us three rooms, washing and cooking and what else we need, we have agreed to give him three crowns a month.

In organizing the counterreformation, Ignatius' chief tactic was preaching. But his followers did not devote much time to preaching in the churches. Rather they concentrated on influencing people who could mold the course of events. In Germany, however, their efforts failed to oust heresy. In that country the people were sharply divided into Catholics and Protestants, due to the different views on doctrine. Lutheranism had a tight grip on many of the people. But the Jesuits succeeded in obstructing what had appeared at one time an unassailable advance of Protestantism. Moreover, they guided back to the Catholic faith many who had been wavering.

Even so, the conversions were not on a spectacular scale, such as, for instance, what Estrada achieved in Portugal, Araoz at Valladolid, Bobadilla at Birignano, and Laínez in Florence.

It is highly probably, however, that Luther would have conquered a far greater religious empire but for such Jesuits as Laínez, Favre, and Le Jay. They reasoned with the princes and lords of the German Diet and disputed publicly with the doctors of the universities who were hostile to Rome.

Even more noteworthy in arresting Luther's attack on papal authority was Peter Canisius. The Holy See had no stronger champion in Germany. As provincial of the Society of Jesus, he was the architect of the Catholic movement that was built up in northern Europe.

CHAPTER 16

THE FINAL YEARS

Religion had been intermingled with politics and war, and Ignatius was only too well aware of the folly of this. He knew that the most vital instrument for Catholic advance was teaching. Therefore, colleges were founded, and the Jesuits also occupied pulpits and university chairs. Crowds of students listened to the Jesuit interpretation of the Scriptures and to their denouncement of the Lutheran claims.

One of the most eminent teaching centers that arose in these times was the German College, founded in Rome in 1552. Catholics could not avoid the fact that Protestantism had thrived on the decadence, ignorance, and corruption of many priests. Some of the clergy had even gone over to the heretics, and a further weakening of the Catholic cause was a decrease in vocations to the priesthood. The shortage was so acute that some fifteen hundred German parishes lacked a single priest.

It was imperative to resolve this problem. But how? The answer came from Cardinal Morone, after visiting Germany as the papal delegate. A new reliable breed of clergy, he considered, was possible only by educating well-selected

German youths. The Cardinal received Ignatius' enthusiastic support, and it was agreed to set up the college in Rome so that Ignatius could supervise it.

Both the pope, now Julius III, and various cardinals approved the plan. The problem was how to finance it. Ignatius had an attractive parchment produced bearing the pope's name, and around it, in the style of a crown, the names of the thirty-two cardinals residing in Rome.

The idea must have appealed to Julius, for he promised to subscribe five hundred scudi yearly. This sum was inscribed beneath the pope's name; then Ignatius sent the parchment to every cardinal, requesting each to contribute as well. It was a wily move. Under the circumstances, one could scarcely decline. The annual sums offered ranged from fifty to two hundred scudi.

With this guaranteed backing, Ignatius secured premises close to the Roman College, which had been established as a gift of Francis Borgia. On August 31, 1552, the new institution officially came into being. The first twenty candidates were greeted by Ignatius on November 19.

Had he lived longer, Ignatius would have introduced another innovation to bolster the Catholic campaign in Germany. During a tour of the Jesuit colleges in northern Europe, Nadal was alarmed by the growth of Protestant literature. On his return he impressed upon Ignatius the urgent need to organize a college of writers to counter the controversial claims of their religious rivals. Ignatius chose Laínez, Andrea Frusis, and other theologians to be the Catholic propagandists, but his death stopped the project.

Both the German and Roman colleges symbolized the importance of education under the Jesuit system. Schools spread across Europe. Actually, the Society set out on its educational career in 1546 by annexing free day schools in all the colleges. By means of the schools and colleges the Jesuits were able to gradually remold religious thinking in Europe.

One salient rule was that non-Catholic children should not be debarred. It was a firm condition, however, that parents or guardians must ask to have their children admitted. A conspicuous example was the Roman College, to which children traveled from all over Europe.

Apart from the high quality of teaching, there was another attraction: Ignatius insisted that no fees could be received by Jesuits. This enabled poor as well as rich scholars to derive benefit. But it put other schools in jeopardy. Schoolmasters who relied on fees for a livelihood were obviously resentful. In the Spanish Netherlands they managed to have the Jesuits banned from their country until after Ignatius' death. Even then the Jesuits functioned only with acute difficulty.

In Rome, some schoolmasters even resorted to violence, on one occasion attacking a Jesuit while he was teaching. As Ignatius was also to discover, there was the risk of aggrieved parents. Once he felt impelled to write to his college rectors that "two boys being missed from their fathers' houses, the mothers came to our chapel during the Mass, and called out and made an astonishing scandal, and also in the college, and at the house of some of the cardinals . . . saying that we had made the college on purpose to steal away people's sons, and that we kept theirs, etc.; and in fact neither of these [boys] had entered either our college or our house. I thought it right to mention these things, as a warning that your reverences may be better prepared for similar accidents. . . .

"Let them take care also that none of the auditors of the schools admit [any pupils] without assent of the parents, because the harm done by the disturbance and alienation of minds would be far greater than the benefit in receiving them. . . ."

The system of teaching that the Jesuits gradually evolved —more so after Ignatius' death—was to dominate European education for two centuries. In some ways modern educational systems have not escaped some effects of that early teaching.

Ignatius fully appreciated the value of shaping and developing the minds of the young. His methods were strongly influenced by his own studies at the University of Paris, as he once explained to a questioner seeking details about day pupils. Stress was placed on morals. According to their capacity, scholars were taught humane letters, Latin, Greek, and even Hebrew. When they were sufficiently advanced, they learned logic and philosophy.

The Society, he further explained, "provides lecturers, who go through the course of arts, and finally that of theology, as they do at Paris. And these not only give lessons, but exercise all the scholars in composition and disputes, and various conferences, which perhaps are more useful than [direct] instruction."

He fostered a love of music and poetry, acting and oratory. As for classical education, it has been claimed that this survived because of the Jesuits. Ignatius was not opposed to the classics, but he resented those authors whose works bred scorn for Christian truth or undermined it. In fact, Igna-

140

tius insisted in education generally that the moral and religious aspects must always overshadow intellectual training.

He had disseminated the faith among infidels, then planted the roots of Jesuit teaching and applied his wisdom in eradicating decadence in the Catholic Church. The counterreformation came at the climax of his life. Yet, despite the immensity of his task, Ignatius could still diligently attend, with characteristic humility, to less complex projects.

In 1543 he had set up the House of St. Martha, a center for wayward women. Some of these people wished to return to normal life but lacked the moral fiber to escape from their sordid surroundings. Those who were able and willing to take the vows could enter the Monastery of St. Madeline. But others—such as married women—were unable to do so. Hence, the House of Martha. But it meant one more strain on the Society's finances.

Ignatius, however, did not alarm himself over such mundane things as money. God, he believed, would in some way always provide. And it is amazing how help sometimes came without warning. As it happened, some old Roman relics—sculptured reliefs and statues—were unearthed in front of the Jesuits' church, and when a lucrative sale was made of the discovery, the money enabled Ignatius to purchase land. The munificence of others allowed the asylum scheme to mature.

Ignatius would sometimes accompany these women through the streets to the new quarters, acts that evoked criticism. Even the windows at the center were smashed by irate people, but Ignatius was undeterred.

Another maligned section of the community was the

141

Jews who lived in a ghetto across the Tiber. On listening to the street preaching of the Jesuits, some were converted, only to be persecuted by their kinsmen if they made a public avowal of their new belief. Those shunned by their families were taken in at the Jesuit house, but when their numbers increased Ignatius set up the House of Catechumens for them.

Most probably to the chagrin of the orthodox Jews, Pope Julius III and Pope Paul IV, who succeeded him, compelled the Italian synagogues to help maintain this center. And Ignatius succeeded in getting rid of a law that deprived these converts of their possessions.

But again, Ignatius' altruism provoked abuse. When slanders emanated from the priest in charge of the House of Catechumens, Ignatius stubbornly insisted that the accusations should be investigated by a proper court.

Fearlessly, Ignatius struck at the social evils of Rome. He established homes for orphan children and St. Catherine's, a sanctuary for girls who might otherwise be victims of the city's corruption.

All the time Ignatius labored despite failing health. On Christmas Day, 1550, while saying Mass, he had a seizure. It seemed that death was near. However, he slowly recovered. But feeling unequal to the duties demanded by the generalship, he dictated a letter to Polanco. This letter, written to the Fathers, suggested that someone should be chosen in his place. Only one of the brethren, Oviedo, agreed; the rest objected to a successor.

From now on, he would never regain good health. Fastings and other privations were taking their toll. There were times when his meager diet was no more than fruit and overripe cheese. As the days went by, the need for help in the administration of the Society grew apparent. Ignatius was not wholeheartedly in favor of it, but in October, 1554, Father Jerome Nadal assumed the duties of vicar-general. This assistance ended after some months. Nadal wanted to introduce more prayer into the colleges, but Ignatius was not in favor of this and so he sent Nadal to Spain.

Ignatius had two more years to live. In that time his life flickered like a flame. As he grew weaker in body he sensed that his life was drawing to a close. But he could reflect on fantastic achievements. From the status of what was no better than that of a humble beggar, he had founded and developed a powerful movement that was exercising influence on countless people, both high and low. Houses, colleges, and missions were thriving in Europe, as well as in India, Africa, and South America. Many more would appear in other countries. The fortunes of his Society would fluctuate in the years ahead, but there would be greater expansion until every race and every category of people would in some way be affected by it.

Therein lies the significance of Saint Ignatius of Loyola. Posterity does not merely appraise him as one of the giants of the sixteenth century; he was one of the most eminent of all time. Whereas the power of many forceful personalities in history ended with their death, the influence of Ignatius —through his Jesuit movement—has continued. He set the concrete foundations of a structure that has withstood the test of four centuries.

A Church militant, with the ill-dressed knights of his

small army he had striven by peaceful conquest to bring men—both in the Old World and the New—into the kingdom of Christ. That work continues.

He believed wholeheartedly in the Catholic Church. He opposed anything that threatened the centuries-old status of the papacy. Yet he was conscious of the reasons for revolt in the Church. Ignatius, therefore, attacked the moral decay as well as the new religion and saved the greater part of Europe for the papacy. To do this he forged a weapon far mightier than the sword: education in the Church, education among laymen.

In taking the banner of Christ into strange lands, some of His sons would risk the hazards of the desert. Others, for the sake of Christian teaching, would die from barbarous treatment. At the time of Ignatius' death the Jesuit army was a thousand strong. Two generations later this religious force would grow to more than thirteen times that figure.

During the summer of 1556, Ignatius became so feeble that the duties of the generalship had to be shared by Polanco, Nadal—returned from Spain—and Christopher Madrid. Ignatius withdrew to a villa in the country, but after some days his fever worsened and he was taken back to Rome. Immediate danger appears to have been discounted by the brethren. Laínez, who was also sick, was thought to be in a more critical state. But Ignatius was dying. Ribadeneira recorded for posterity the scene at the end.

Late on the afternoon of July 30, 1556—"about the third hour before sundown"—Ignatius summoned Polanco, and though speaking with composure, said: "Master Polanco, the hour of my departure from this world is at hand. Go in my behalf and kiss His Holiness' feet, and ask for his blessing, and to go with it a plenary indulgence for all my sins; so that I may face this life in greater comfort and confidence; and tell His Holiness that if I—for I trust in God's infinite mercy—shall find myself on the Holy Mount of His glory, I shall not forget to pray for His Holiness, as I have always done every time that I have felt constrained to pray for myself."

Polanco, both surprised and puzzled, replied: "Father, the doctors do not regard your illness as dangerous, and for my part I hope that God will leave your reverence for His better service with us for several years still. Do you think you are as ill as Laínez?"

"So sick," answered Ignatius, "that there is no more to do but die."

Still believing in the doctors' judgment, Polanco asked if he might wait till the following day. He wanted to send some letters to Spain by the post for Genoa that evening.

Ignatius answered: "I should like today better than tomorrow, the sooner the better. But do what you think best. I leave it to you."

Polanco waited to ascertain if the doctors believed him to be in danger, and sent for the head doctor, Master Alexander, asking him to tell him frankly what he thought. Polanco also said that he was charged with an errand to the pope. Alexander answered: "I can't say anything today; tomorrow we'll see."

Under the circumstances, because Ignatius had left the decision to him, Polanco waited to hear the doctor's view the following day. That same Thursday, about eight o'clock in the evening, Doctor Madrid and Polanco took supper

145

with Ignatius. He ate as usual and chatted. And so Polanco left the room without a thought of fatality. But at daybreak he found Ignatius on the point of death.

Polanco ran to St. Peter's. The pope expressed great sorrow and blessed Ignatius with all possible affection. Less than two hours before sunrise, in the presence of Dr. Madrid and André Desfreux, Ignatius of Loyola peacefully gave up his soul to God. He was sixty-five years of age.

Many people came to see the dead Ignatius as he lay in state in the place where he died. Some kissed his feet or hands or touched his body with their rosaries. Some attempted to take momentoes, even pieces of his biretta. And although he had declined similar requests in his lifetime, several portraits were allowed to be made.

After Vespers on the evening of August 1, Ignatius was interred in a wooden coffin in his beloved Santa Maria della Strada. The body would be removed twelve years later when the new great Church of Jesus rose majestically on the site. That, then, would be his final resting-place—in the main chapel to the right of the altar.

The general had fought his last campaign for the greater glory of God. As a Jesuit would write many years later, he had "stood for the cause of his holy Church, and the rebirth of piety and holiness of life, wherever the glory of the Christian name had been tarnished." But perhaps the simplest and most telling words are the ones inscribed on his tomb: Ignatio, Societatis Jesu Fundatori—Ignatius, Founder of the Society of Jesus.

EVENTS IN THE LIFE OF
SAINT IGNATIUS

1491	Ignatius is born at the castle of Loyola.
1517	His patron, Juan Veláquez de Cuéllar, dies; he enters the service of the Duke of Nájera.
1521	Is wounded at Pamplona, and is converted.
1522	Keeps vigil at Montserrat, March 24; goes to Manresa where he writes the *Spiritual Exercises*.
1523	Leaves for Barcelona and begins pilgrimage to Jerusalem.
1524	Starts his studies in Barcelona.
1526–27	Becomes student at the universities of Alcalá and Salamanca.
1528	Arrives at the University of Paris.
1534	With first disciples, takes the vow at Montmartre, Paris, to engage in apostolic service.
1535	Returns to Spain and visits Azpeitia for the last time.
1537	Arrives in Venice; travels from Venice to Rome and offers the services of his Society to the pope.

1540   Paul III issues a papal bull and the Society of Jesus begins its eventful career as an official order.

1541   As the Society's first general, Ignatius makes his vow of obedience to the pope in the Church of St. Paul, Rome, April 22.

1546   Sends representatives to the Council of Trent.

1548   Pope Paul III approves the *Spiritual Exercises*.

1550   The constitutions are finally sanctioned by Pope Julius III.

1551   The Roman College is founded.

1556   Ignatius dies in Rome.

1662   Ignatius is canonized.

INDEX